1859
in Review

NP WESTMINSTER, MARYLAND

THOMAS P. NEILL, Ph.D.

Department of History, St. Louis University

1859
in Review

The Newman Press • 1959

Nihil obstat: REV. DAVID T. THOMAS, J.C.D.
                  Censor Librorum

Imprimatur: JOSEPH E. RITTER, S.T.D.
                  Archbishop of St. Louis

                  October 27, 1959

Preface

THE following essays attempt to trace in broad strokes the development of certain important trends of the last century. They are based not on immediate, individual research for each topic, but rather on knowledge and reflection that comes from repeatedly covering this ground with graduate and undergraduate students over the last two decades.

Although each essay is on a different topic and is a unit, nevertheless the subjects are all interconnected and even entangled in many ways. Underlying them is a unity not only of time and place, but also of flavor and development. For each trend is a thread of the same tapestry, the historical cloth of the last century. The topics serve as seven vantage points from which the last century can be viewed, and perhaps they will suggest to the reader a glimpse of the direction history seems to be taking in our generation.

It is impossible for one who studies the last century thoroughly and re-examines it repeatedly to emerge either an unqualified optimist or a complete pessimist. For there are hopeful portents among the ominous, and no historian has the gift of prophecy to foretell which will prevail. The author of these essays, the reader should be advised, considers himself a restrained, qualified optimist who has not found in the annals of history a perfect society to which we should return, nor one so confused and corrupt that tough human nature did not somehow survive it.

The following essays were all done originally for this volume. The author borrowed some paragraphs from the essays on Darwin and Dewey in the last edition of his *Makers of the Modern Mind* (Milwaukee, Wisconsin: Bruce Publishing Co., 1958), with the kind permission of the publisher. I also wish to express my gratitude to the following publishers for their kind permissions to quote copyrighted material: Columbia University Press for *France: A Nation of Patriots,* by Carlton J. H. Hayes (New York, 1929); Crown Publishers for *Karl Marx: The Story of His Life,* by Franz Mehring (New York, 1935); The University of Chicago Press for *The Logic of Liberty,* by Michael Polanyi (Chicago, 1951; originally published as an essay in *Measure,* 1950).

Contents

Introduction:

1859 in Retrospect

SOME YEARS are eventful. Seventeen hundred and seventy-six is known to every American as the year of the Declaration of Independence, to Californians as the date of the founding of San Francisco, to students of history as the year also in which Adam Smith published his *Wealth of Nations*. Every English schoolboy knows 1758 as "annus mirabilis," the year in which William Pitt turned defeat into victory in England's war against France. Other historical dates are known by all who can read and write— for example, "1066 and all that"; 1492, when "Columbus sailed the ocean blue"; and 1848, when all Europe blazed into revolution and civil wars.

Eighteen hundred and fifty-nine appears an unusually eventful year in the perspective of a century. To people who lived through that year it may have seemed much like 1858 or 1860, but we know now that it was an unusually productive year and that it can well be called "annus propheticus" or "annus fecundus." In 1859, for example, Karl Marx published his *Critique of Political Economy*, which contains the fundamental ideas in his later and more famous *Das Kapital,* and shows forth a doctrine and a prophecy which have guided millions in their revolutions still being waged over a large part of the globe. Later in the same year Charles Darwin published his *Origin of Species,* which came to be identified with evolution and did much to change the way men think about themselves and about history.

Not only books but also men destined to guide the course of history in the last century were born in 1859. This is the year of John Dewey's birth, and no one has influenced education so much in recent times as this New England-born philosopher. In this same year the future discoverer of radium, Pierre Curie, was born in France; in Germany was born the man destined to lead his country into the first World War, the future Kaiser Wilhelm II. Thus 1859 appears as a year of beginnings, a year giving birth to men and ideas destined to play important roles in the drama of history through the following century.

A necrology of the year suggests that the old order was passing away in 1859. The architect of that order, Prince Klemens von Metternich, died on June 11. As host to the powers that had defeated

Napoleon, von Metternich controlled the Congress of Vienna and dominated Europe for the first half of the century. He was preceded in death three weeks by Ferdinand II of Naples, the personification of everything wretched and despicable in the absolutist monarchies. In April, Alexis de Tocqueville had died, a man who personified the best aspects of the Old Regime but who was nonetheless attached to it by birth and sentiment.

Movements and institutions associated with the old order of things also died in 1859. An attempt to restore the old absolutism in Spain died a-borning when the Spanish army refused to support Don Carlos Luis against his relatively liberal cousin, Queen Isabella. In England the Peelite Conservatives disbanded to form the modern Liberal Party, and the Conservative government of Lord Derby was defeated in Parliament and at the polls. A Liberal government under the fiery Palmerston came to power and inaugurated policies typical of the century following 1859. Culturally as well as politically it seemed that an old age was passing away. Thomas Babington Macaulay died in England and Washington Irving passed away in America. Each was associated in the popular mind with a period in letters then coming to an end, while younger men were inaugurating a new era. Former outstanding thinkers also died on the European continent, such as the famed naturalist Alexander von Humboldt, and Karl Ritter, generally considered the founder of modern geography.

As the passing of an old order was marked by deaths in 1859, so was the beginning of a new order marked by significant births. Besides Wilhelm II, Curie, and Dewey, many other persons destined for greatness first saw the light of day in 1859. Among them were Jean Jaurès and Sidney Webb. Both were influenced by Karl Marx and, although neither was a Communist, each did much to spread Socialist doctrine and institutions, Jaurès as a prominent French politician and Webb as historian of the working class in England. Henri Bergson was also born in this year. By the end of the century he had put into philosophical form new ideas about the nature of life, evolution, and reality, and he exerted considerable influence on such diverse philosophers as John Dewey, Alfred North Whitehead, and Jacques Maritain. Other celebrated persons born in 1859 were Alfred Dreyfus, destined to be the central figure in the most famous trial in modern French history, and Eleonora Duse, perhaps the most celebrated actress of all time.

The year 1859 is not all ends and beginnings. In that year two men—born on the same day of February 12, 1809—reached their fiftieth birthday and took steps that made them internationally famous in the following year. These men were Abraham Lincoln and Charles Darwin, who were soon to be leading figures respectively in the American Civil War and the great "monkey-battle" over man's origin. Perhaps "significant change" would be a more accurate label to attach to 1859 than "end" or "beginning." In that year, for example, the British completed the dissolution of the East India Company and inaugurated a new form of imperialism that has been followed till today. No longer were missionary ardor and reforming zeal to characterize British imperialist policy, but rather a detached, impersonal, efficient administration of imperial affairs. Reform and missionary zeal were to be restricted to missionaries and not to be part of governmental policy.

Another significant change in 1859 was the conversion of Gladstone from the Conservative to the Liberal Party. As Liberal leader for over a quarter of a century, Gladstone effected many reforms in England and inaugurated a more humane policy toward Ireland. In this same year the last religious group suffering political disabilities in England—the

Jews—were emancipated by a law which provided an oath that they could conscientiously take for admittance to Parliament. Perhaps the most important significant political change of the year occurred in France. Eighteen hundred and fifty-nine marked the end of the personal rule of Napoleon III and the beginning of the so-called "Liberal Empire." Because his participation in the War of Italian Liberation lost him support among both Catholics and Liberals, Napoleon III tried to consolidate his domestic position with political concessions. The first of these was a full amnesty, on August 19, to all men in prison for political offenses.

The best title for 1859, however, is "annus propheticus," for the year is replete with incidents prophetic of important trends and events of the following century. One of these, insignificant as it might seem in 1959, is a steep increase in the income tax as a method of balancing the budget in England. Tax on income was rather new in 1859, but by 1959 it has become the chief means of both financing the government and redistributing wealth, in England and many other countries. In 1859 England and France negotiated the Cobden commercial treaty, which was a long step in the direction of free trade between these two countries. This treaty was strongly supported by Liberal leaders, such as Gladstone, who were destined to control so many countries' futures in 1859. In other countries, such as Spain, there was serious labor unrest, with general strikes revealing a rebellious class to which Marxian doctrine would soon make a strong appeal.

There were other straws in the wind suggestive of future developments. On December 22, more than a decade before the creation of the Roman Question,* Napoleon III published under a pseudonym a pamphlet, *The Pope and the Congress,* in which he proposed conditions on which the Vatican state is now based. In this same year events in the Americas suggested what was forthcoming. England, France, and Spain took the typical imperialist step of seizing the port of Vera Cruz in Mexico, to collect customs duties in payment of debts which the revolutionary government of Benito Juárez had renounced. This strong-fist policy was recognized by the use, for the first time in 1859, of the word "imperialist" and the counter-allegation of "anti-imperialist."

The forthcoming Civil War in the United States

* The Roman Question was created when Italy took Rome from the Pope in 1870. The Pope refused to admit the validity of this seizure, and he remained a voluntary prisoner in the Vatican Palace until the Question was settled in 1929.

was presaged in 1859 by John Brown's raid on Harper's Ferry. This fantastic scheme to free slaves by raids from a fortified rendezvous in the mountains of Virginia was frustrated by Colonel Robert E. Lee. Brown was captured, found guilty of treason and executed, and within a short time northern soldiers were marching south to the tune of:

"John Brown's body lies a-mouldering in the grave, But his soul goes marching on."

The first step toward another civil war was taken in the same year when the Prussian king ordered complete mobilization of his army, sent Otto von Bismarck as ambassador to Russia, and appointed General von Roon minister of war. Bismarck and Roon were destined to reform the Prussian army and lead Prussia into war against Austria and to the unification of Germany in the next decade.

The coming age of imperialism and industrialism was pointed to with prophetic fingers by a number of events in 1859. On April 25, the first spadeful of earth was turned over in the digging of the Suez Canal, which a century later remains a sore spot in international relationships. A telegraph cable between England and India was completed in this same year, a step which, like the Suez Canal, short-ened distances and made world-wide imperialism feasible for the first time. Tungsten steel was first manufactured in Germany in 1859, and the first commercial oil field was discovered in Pennsylvania. Both events presaged remarkable developments to come in the oil and steel industries, for oil made possible the automotive and airplane industries and led nations to struggle for sources of supply, and tung-sten steel made possible new machinery, boilers, shells, and tools requiring a harder steel than was available before 1859.

Even more important were the strong stirrings of nationalism in 1859. There were manifestations of nationalism almost everywhere this year. Let us ob-serve these in only two countries. In one of them, Prussia, it soon attained its objective of an inde-pendent national state; in the other, Ireland, it led to nothing but heartache and failure until the twen-tieth century. Throughout Prussia the centenary of Schiller's birth was celebrated with song festivals and highly nationalistic programs. The Prussian govern-ment smiled benignly on such festivities, whereas earlier in the nineteenth century it had frowned on them as dangerous and revolutionary. In this same year Gustav Freytag began the publication of his six volumes of sketches of German life since the Middle Ages. These too were highly nationalistic, designed to stir up pride among Germans and create a moving desire for national unity. Liberal statesmen organized the *Deutscher-Nationalverein* to work for national unification in 1859.

A similar story was unfolding in Ireland, but here a tragic note prevailed. In 1859 the Phoenix Society was suppressed by the British as a conspiracy to overthrow English rule and attain independence. Its founder John Stephens, who had been a leader of several independence movements, visited America to enlist support and obtain funds for his struggle. Stephens and his associates named their new association the Fenian Brotherhood, a group whose members took an illegal oath to work for independence. The name of the new organization stirred up nationalist feelings in Irish hearts, for it reminded them of Ireland's past glories, of the legendary Feni, companions of Fionn, the son of Coul, whose deeds were the marvel of pre-historic Ireland and were to be imitated in the nineteenth century. Other events with a nationalistic bent in Ireland were the founding of the National Gallery to cultivate national consciousness among the Irish, and constant agitation against the National School System controlled by the English.

Not all things begun in 1859 were prophetic of success. John Henry Newman, for example, was asked to take over the editorship of a Catholic journal, *The Rambler*. Newman proposed that his aim for *The Rambler* was "to create a body of thought as against the false intellectualism of the age, to surround Catholicism with defenses necessary for and demanded by the age, to take a Catholic view of and give a Catholic interpretation to the discoveries of the age." The English bishops feared that such a bold venture would undermine their authority, and in July they asked Newman to resign. A century later bishops in both England and America are endeavoring to achieve precisely what Newman asked for in 1859.

To the average Englishman of 1859 the most important event of the year must have seemed the sinking in the English Channel of the steamer *Royal Charter* coming from Australia. 445 persons were lost, as well as a million pounds of gold. A second most important event would probably have seemed the "Great Panic," when Englishmen were seized with fear that Napoleon III might invade the country. Thousands of volunteers enlisted in the militia, were armed by the government, and drilled so as to become an effective force to defend the country.

1859 seemed threatened by war clouds. An author wrote in *Bentley's Quarterly Review*: "The Horizon is already darkening. . . . Cuba, Nicaragua, the valley of the Po and Danube, any of them may be the scene of conflict that will force England into war. On the decision of England will hang the happiness of millions, and perhaps the future of civilization itself." In similar vein a writer in *Littell's Living Age* observed: "That this is a time of agitation we presume none will deny. It is obvious that the key of the question lies in the policy of England. . . . She is certainly called upon to decide whether it shall be a duel between two great powers settling old differences on an historical battlefield or a general war in which the very interests of civilization may be imperiled."

The more observing Englishman would have been concerned with war clouds gathering on the continent. On the first day of the year, at his customary New Year's Day reception for foreign diplomats, Napoleon III created a sensation by turning

on the Austrian Ambassador Hübner and saying, "I
am sorry that the relations between us are so unsat-
isfactory." Ten days later the king of Sardinia-Pied-
mont, Victor Emmanuel II, told his Parliament:

The horizon on which the New Year opens is not
quite clear. . . . Our country, small as it is, has become influential in the councils of Europe, because of
the greatness of the ideas which she represents, and of
the sympathies which she inspires. The situation is not
exempt from danger, for, while respecting treaties, we
cannot disregard the cry of grief which rises to us from
so many parts of Italy. Strong in union, confident in
our right, we await with prudence and resolution the
decrees of Providence.

This call to arms was answered by its hearers with
wild applause. On January 30 the emperor's cousin,
Jérôme Bonaparte, married Princess Clotilde, daughter of Victor Emmanuel II, a marriage interpreted
as cementing an alliance between these countries
against Austria.

Thus, before the first month of 1859 had passed,
intelligent observers could see that war was brewing
and that the mixture was likely to explode before the
year was done.

Meanwhile, a number of important books and

operas were produced which were destined to have a greater lasting effect on the following century than the War of Italian Liberation. The most effective events of 1859, indeed, were the appearance of works of the mind. Among the notable English books to appear in this year were Charles Dickens' *Tale of Two Cities*, George Eliot's first important novel, *Adam Bede*, George Meredith's *The Ordeal of Richard Feveral*, Edward Fitzgerald's translation of the *Rubáiyát of Omar Khayyám*, and Alfred Tennyson's *Idylls of the King*, all works still read by students of English literature. In France Victor Hugo published his *La Légende des Siècles*, and in Germany Gustav Freytag began publication of his six-volume nationalistic study of German life in the past. Gounod's *Faust* had its premiere performance in Paris on March 19, and a new form of dramatic opera was inaugurated in Germany with Wagner's *Tristan and Isolde*.

A number of epoch-making works appeared in 1859 which are deserving of special attention because of their effects in the past century, works which are given centenary commemoration this year.

1. The first of these is Charles Darwin's *Origin of Species*. Published on November 24, Darwin's

work was an immediate success. The original edition of twelve hundred and fifty copies was sold on the first day, and within a month the publisher was running off a second edition of three thousand copies. The *Origin* quickly became the best selling scientific work in the history of the English language, going through six editions and selling forty thousand copies in England alone in Darwin's lifetime, in addition to many pirated editions in this and other countries. Darwin's book was soon mistakenly identified with evolution, and about it there came to be much misunderstanding and absurd controversy. It forced fundamentalists in religion to rethink their position or to withdraw into intellectual isolation. It was applied and misapplied to many areas of speculation to justify war, ruthless competition in business, and an optimistic view of the "benefits" of starvation, the early death of weaklings in the "struggle for survival," and the failure of the "less fit" businesses and nations against their more successful competitors. The *Origin of Species* is a book, then, which had tremendous effect in making the world what it is a century after it was published.

2. Earlier in 1859, Karl Marx published his *Zur Kritik der Politischen Ökonomie* in Berlin. Unlike Darwin's work, Marx's was not popularly received.

Marx complained that the bourgeoisie "tried to kill my works by silence," and his daughter Laura wrote of the "conspiracy of silence" that kept the *Critique of Political Economy* under wraps. But these are merely excuses. Even Marx's closest friend, Friedrich Engels, admitted that he found the work very difficult to understand. One of Marx's most sympathetic biographers, Franz Mehring, explains of this work:

> In the beginning, the flood of light generated by this critical examination dazzled even the friends of the author more than it enlightened them. Liebnecht declared that he had never been so much disappointed by a work before, and Miquel found "very little actually new" in it. . . . If that was the reception Marx's work had at the hands of those who might have been expected to understand it, what could be expected of others? . . . Indeed, how should a world which had enthroned money as its God aspire to understand it?

The *Critique of Political Economy*, which contained the essence of Marxian doctrine, acted like a delayed-action bomb. It was incorporated as the first chapters of *Das Kapital*, and had its effect on Europe and the rest of the world only after Marx's death some quarter of a century later. Since then Marxian teaching has played an important role in modifying social and economic thought everywhere, as well as inspiring revolution throughout a good part of the world.

3. In February, one of the outstanding thinkers in England published a work which was considered somewhat old-fashioned in 1859, the essay *On Liberty,* on which he and his wife had labored for several years. John Stuart Mill and his wife had worked and re-worked this essay several times before her untimely death in 1858. Early the following year, Mill published the work without further alteration. *On Liberty* was not designed to be a popular book. It was read by influential, intellectual people and it made its mark through them. Nevertheless, a cheaper edition was published in 1865, and within a week it sold over a thousand copies.

A century later, *On Liberty* remains one of the classic defenses of personal freedom, a defense that has lost none of its cogency after a century of industrialization, of technological progress, of increasing state power, and of a definite trend away from individualism. It is a document whose light has sometimes grown dim but has never gone out. It deserves examination not only for its influence and for its cogency today, but also for its weaknesses, for there is good reason to feel that a new and better plea for human liberty in modern times is needed than the one John Stuart Mill made so eloquently a hundred years ago. The light of liberty seems to need stronger batteries than Mill gave it a century ago.

4. In 1859, Dr. Samuel Smiles published his *Self Help*, a work which enjoyed remarkable popularity at once. It was translated into seventeen languages; some Japanese students are said to have memorized the entire book, and a Mohammedan gentleman to have lined his wall with quotations from it, alongside excerpts from the Koran. A few reviews were critical of *Self Help*, but it struck the right tune for the times, as Darwin did in the field of science, and it was read by millions. Smiles received thousands of letters of thanks for the encouragement he had given readers with his message that "perseverance and courage would, in the end, lead to success of the best sort."

Smiles had been invited to lecture on "self-improvement" for a group of serious young working-men who were trying to "get ahead" by reading and self-education. His lectures were enlivened by hundreds of examples of men who had "made good," and this seems to have been the chief appeal of the book. In it were condensed all the ideas later popularized in this country by Horatio Alger, Jr. *Self Help* epitomized the thought of middle class Liberalism: individualistic self-sufficiency is the hallmark of a worthwhile man; frugality, sobriety, and industry are always rewarded by success; one who falls by the wayside deserves no sympathy, since failure is just punishment for indolence and wastefulness; there is a divine economy whereby each gets what he deserves. This philosophy lay behind great accomplishments in the years after 1859, and it underlay much concomitant misery. It was subjected to severe criticism by Socialists and by religious groups, and it gave ground before a swelling popular reaction. But it has never entirely died out. There are still men of substance in the United States who say that economic laws work as impersonally as the tides, and that justice will be done to all and the welfare of all somehow achieved in a free economy where each man may follow his self-interest. And these men still run selections from *Self Help* in their journals to edify their readers and to shame advocates of the welfare state.

5. In 1859, the small state of Piedmont launched its drive to unify Italy by starting the War of Italian Liberation against Austria. The drive was ultimately successful, and a new national state came into being. Since that date of 1859 nationalism has been one of

the most potent forces in history. It has driven men to martyrdom and to heresy, to noble sacrifice and to vile hatred. It has complicated politics and international relations. It has flavored music and infected literature. It played a large part in bringing about and intensifying two world wars. And it has tended to make rational peace settlements impossible.

6. In 1859, when the English army finally put down the Sepoy Mutiny, great celebrations were held throughout England. The Indian rebellion led the English government to suppress the East India Company in the previous year, take over that company's holdings in 1858 and 1859, and inaugurate a new form of imperialism. In this same year, a new war was begun against the Chinese because they refused to abide by the humiliating terms of the treaty ending the recent "Arrow War." In succeeding decades, imperialism became one of the dominant factors in history. It went through a cycle of European penetration into "backward" countries, their division into "spheres of influence," their economic and industrial exploitation, the emergence of a native class of leaders, and their eventual securing of independence. Today, a century after the suppression of the Sepoy Mutiny, imperialism has gone through its full cycle, and it is proper to speak of the "twilight of imperialism." Meanwhile, European culture and in-

dustrial know-how have spread into the more populous areas of Asia and Africa, and Europe is losing its dominant position in the world. With imperialism, moreover, there has spread throughout the world a knowledge of European ideas and religions which may in mid-twentieth century be inaugurating a new chapter in history.

7. In 1859, Herbert Spencer published the last of four essays on education, "What Knowledge is of Most Worth?" Published later in book form, Spencer's essays on education became a popular seller, especially in the United States, and played a leading role in the great battle of education still being fought in 1959 and probably destined never to be finally settled. Writing in 1859, Spencer sounds almost like a slick-magazine author today with his demand for education in science as against languages and the liberal arts. Spencer undoubtedly had influence in the rapid introduction of science into the educational curriculum in the decades after his studies were published.

We have observed that in 1859 the first commercial oil field was developed in Pennsylvania, and tungsten steel was produced commercially in Germany. In the century since these developments, industrial progress in the United States, Germany, and the entire world has centered around oil and steel as much as anything. The growth of the automobile industry, the development of air, truck, and bus travel at the expense of the railroad, the growth of oil and gas heating, and all the achievements made possible by structural steel are significant industrial changes which affect every aspect of our lives and have had a profound influence on international relations in the last century. The development of each of the ideas enumerated above, then, took place in the matrix of a rapidly developing industrial society and an accompanying machine-oriented mentality.

Each of these events or books let loose a powerful idea in 1859 that influenced history throughout the last century. And through the century each of these ideas changed form and substance as it gained momentum, met counter-forces, or ran into stubborn opposition. For those who are intellectually curious, who "like history," as well as those who desire a more penetrating understanding of the factors which made the world what it is in 1959, it is helpful to have a description of the life course of these ideas and forces which are now a hundred years from their launching: Darwinism, Marxism, individualism, liberalism, nationalism, imperialism, and trust in education.

1859
in Review

Chapter I

Evolution Through a Hundred Years

IT IS generally agreed by historians of ideas that Darwin's *Origin of Species* was the most important book of 1859, perhaps of the entire nineteenth century, for as Father J. Franklin Ewing, S.J., put it a century later, it "was the spark which initiated a great explosion in the history of thought. It was Darwin who made evolution a part of modern life." Darwin's *Origin* had an effect out of all proportion to its intrinsic worth, but it struck the right note for the age and caused sympathetic vibrations in practically every study and walk of life.

Darwin was neither a great mind nor a powerful writer. Nor does he stand among the dozen greatest scientists of history. He simply happened to say what the age wanted to hear, and he said it in terms that pleased the age's ear. Darwin spoke of struggle for existence, survival of the fittest, competition for world resources, rapid increase of population, and all those other things the nineteenth century believed in so firmly. He mirrored the age's mentality perfectly, saying what was already believed, but putting it all together in a single pattern under a Master Idea: survival of the fittest through natural selection. This is the secret of Darwin's popularity. This is why he became *the* theorist of evolution, when other equally good explanations were overlooked or rejected.

Jacques Barzun has well said that "Darwin may be said with a slight exaggeration to have found the right wrong idea for cementing together in the minds of his contemporaries the elements of doctrine which had repeatedly been proposed along separate lines of thought." This is why Darwin's contemporaries looked upon him as another Newton, England's second precious gift to the scientific world. Alfred Wallace, who discovered the key idea of natural selection independently of Darwin, called him "the Newton of Natural History." Thomas Huxley drove this idea home by comparing the men personally, by putting the *Origin of Species* alongside Newton's *Principia* in importance and in grandeur. The English people prided themselves on Darwin as they had on Newton. They rewarded him, like Newton, in his own lifetime: they made him a Fellow of the Royal Society and an honorary member of the Royal Society of Edin-

burgh; they bestowed the Copley Medal on him in
1864, and they buried him in Westminster Abbey.

Darwin's importance lay in his having arranged in a systematic pattern what hundreds of predecessors had discovered, and having it all make sense in the light of the Master Idea of survival of the fittest in the struggle for existence through the process of natural selection. This prompted Huxley to assert that from Aristotle's time to his own "there is nothing comparable to the *Origin of Species*, as a connected survey of the phenomena of life permeated and vivified by a central idea."

Darwin is popularly, though mistakenly, thought of as inventor or discoverer of evolution. He neither discovered it nor proved it. As a matter of fact, he did not even use the word "evolution" in the first edition of the *Origin*. He did two things for evolution: first, he amassed evidence to support the general evolutionary theory, which had been propounded in various ways by any number of men before him; second, and most important, he offered a formula to show how evolution could have proceeded by centering his observations around the central fact of natural selection. Evolution sneaks into the *Origin* by the back door, for Darwin's concern was only to account for the origin of individual species by means of natural selection. That is why he originally planned to call the book *Natural Selection,* and only reluctantly allowed the publisher to change the title.

Evolution was in the air in 1859. Any number of respected authors had touched on the subject in the eighteenth and early nineteenth centuries. Lamarck and Darwin's grandfather, Erasmus Darwin, had worked out schemes to explain how all species evolved from a single origin through variation and transmission of these variations to offspring. They had stressed the role of environment in changing habits, and the latter in changing the organism. Others, such as W. E. Wells and Patrick Mathew, had written of natural selection. By 1842, Charles Darwin had sketched a thirty-page draft of his theory, but another seventeen years elapsed before he published it as the *Origin of Species.*

He was driven to publication when Alfred Wallace wrote a paper putting forth the same ideas. By mutual agreement, Wallace's essay and Darwin's sketch were read to the Linnean Society by its secretary on July 1, 1858, and in this way the theory of natural selection was announced to the world. By October, Darwin's manuscript had grown into a small volume, and by the end of the year it had become a five-hundred page book which was to be entitled *An Abstract of an Essay on the Origin of Species and Varieties Through Natural Selection*. On the recommendation of the famous geologist Lyell, John Murray had agreed to publish Darwin's work sight unseen, but when the manuscript arrived its size and its argument aroused serious misgivings on Murray's part. He was sure that the work was too long and dull; he was convinced, moreover, that its central thesis was absurd. So he suggested that Darwin rewrite the manuscript, confining himself to his observations on pigeons, for "everybody is interested in pigeons." Darwin refused, and Murray proceeded with the original manuscript. On November 24, 1859, the long delayed *Origin of Species* appeared. The entire edition of 1250 copies was sold on the first day, and Darwin stood on the threshold of fame. He began work on a new edition at once, and before the year was finished, the presses were rolling off a second edition of 3000 copies. By 1885 more than 40,000 copies were sold in England alone, thousands of copies in both official and pirated editions in America, and translations into Spanish, Czech, Polish, Russian, Hebrew, and almost every tongue. When the sixth English edition appeared in 1872, five German editions had been published, four French, three Russian, and three American, besides the pirated editions. The *Origin of Species* had become one of the world's "Great Books."

Significantly its full title is *The Origin of Species by Means of Natural Selection, or the Preservation of Favored Races in the Struggle for Life.* "This whole volume," Darwin says in his concluding chapter, "is one long argument," a point overlooked by those who consider Darwin the ideal man of science. In it he amasses circumstantial evidence in favor of evolution, but he does not present any positive proof that the theory is true. It is a book which need not be read to be talked about. It need not even be read from cover to cover to be understood and appreciated, for the whole argument is presented in a masterly summary in the last chapter. One need only read the first few chapters and the last, dipping occasionally into the others to see what kind of evidence Darwin adduces to support his general theories.

The first five chapters contain the fundamentals of Darwin's theory. The next four discuss possible objections to his theory; chapters ten to thirteen deal with geology, the geographic distribution of plants and animals, classification, morphology, and embryology in the light of the fundamental theories presented in the first five chapters; the fourteenth chapter is a recapitulation of the argument, where Darwin discards the boots of plodding science to put on poet's wings for a majestic, sweeping flight into the rarefied atmosphere of pure literature.

It is interesting to contemplate a tangled bank [he concludes], clothed with many plants of many kinds, with birds singing on the bushes, with various insects flitting about, and with worms crawling through the damp earth, and to reflect that these elaborately constructed forms, so different from each other, and dependent upon each other in so complex a manner, have all been produced by laws acting around us. These laws, taken in the largest sense, being Growth with Reproduction; Inheritance which is almost implied by reproduction; Variability from the indirect and direct action of the conditions of life, and from use and disuse: A Ratio of Increase so high as to lead to a Struggle for Life, and as a consequence to Natural Selection, entailing Divergence of Character and the Extinction of less-improved forms. Thus, from the war of nature, from famine and death, the most exalted object which we are capable of conceiving, namely, the production of the higher animals, directly follows. There is grandeur in this view of life, with its several powers, having been originally breathed by the Creator into a few forms or into one; and what, whilst this planet has gone cycling on according to the fixed law of gravity, from so simple a beginning endless forms most beautiful and most wonderful have been and are being evolved.

This book is imposing. Its very size is enough to convince many readers. The fact that Darwin raised every possible objection, some of which he could not answer, convinces many others of his objectivity. The mass of evidence from the geological record, from domestic experiments, from geography and from embryology, bears down upon the average reader to crush his resistance as the weight of the sea crushes the life out of a man pulled to the floor of the ocean. But Darwin was right in saying that it is one long argument. It is an argument in favor of the thesis stated by the title, an argument supported by five hundred pages of detailed evidence Darwin had accumulated over the space of almost thirty years. The *Origin* was a powerful book because it was an abstract of a greater, more detailed work yet to come, because it seemed to be so objective, because it was Science speaking—and Science was infallible in 1859.

Darwin approaches the proof of his thesis logically, step by step, handling one point at a time. His first step is to prove that "under domestication we see much variability." He notes three principal points about variation under domestication: (a) it is large in amount; (b) it is inherited; (c) it is not caused by man. Step two is to apply these conclusions to species in the state of nature. "There is no reason why the principles which have acted so efficiently under domestication should not have acted under nature," where, he therefore concludes, variation also occurs. This brings us to the third step: struggle for existence.

A struggle for existence inevitably follows from the high rate at which all organic beings tend to increase. . . . As more individuals are produced than can possibly survive, there must in every case be a struggle for existence, either one individual with another of the same species, or with the individuals of distinct species, or with the physical conditions of life. . . . There is no exception to the rule that every organic being naturally increases at so high a rate, that, if not destroyed the earth would soon be covered by the progeny of a single pair.

From this comes the fourth and crucial step— Darwin's distinct contribution to the theory of evolution. In the struggle for existence, some survive and some fall by the wayside. What determines which will survive and which will not? Darwin answered this question by showing how alterations in the organism occur from time to time, and how some of these alterations enable the organism to adapt itself more perfectly to its environment. These can be called "favorable variations." A white rabbit, for example, will be better adapted for survival in snowy regions than his brown brothers—so in time the brown rabbits will all be exterminated by predatory animals, whereas the white rabbits will have escaped detection and will go on living and reproducing. Or some parent animal of the present giraffe had a long-necked offspring one day who was better equipped to eat top leaves from the trees, so he survived drought years when his shorter-necked brethren perished. His progeny, of course, inherited this favorable variation, and so the giraffe survived as a long-necked animal. What caused the "favorable" variation—the white rabbit or the long neck—was purely a matter of chance.

Thus the fittest survive. And the agency determining their survival is called "natural selection." In later editions of the *Origin of Species,* Darwin gave an increasingly large part to such other agencies as use and disuse, and the direct action of environment, but he always insisted that the dominant role was played by natural selection. These variations, each one slight in itself, add up until there is sufficient change to call the altered animal or plant a new species. Thus the origin of species is explained. And this was all Darwin sought to explain, for he did not deal with the origin of life, as is popularly believed, but rather with the origin and extinction of different forms of life called "species."

The difficulty with Darwin's thesis is that it does not show how species originate, but only how they become extinct. That the fittest survive through natural selection, if this be true, asserts that selection occurs only after the useful change has occurred. This can account for the survival of some and the extinction of others, but not for the origin of a new species. Here Darwin must have recourse to almost measureless time and to the assumption that an infinite series of small variations add up to a large enough change to account for a new species.

It is obvious after a century that Darwin wrote a book that was more important than its contents, for behind it was the force of ideas generating throughout the earlier half of the century. The accumulated force of these ideas, each of which had remained more or less isolated before 1859, was concentrated for the first time in a single work. The *Origin* was consequently an explosive work in its power. Huxley observed with slight exaggeration that "it is doubtful if any single book, except perhaps the *Principia,* ever worked so great and so rapid a revolution in science, or made so deep an impression on the general mind."

So Darwin found himself suddenly famous. Bunbury noted in March of 1860 that "Darwin's book has made a greater sensation than any strictly scientific book that I remember. It is wonderful how much it is talked about by unscientific people." Darwin became the center around which a man-made tempest raged. He was a hero or a villain, a martyr for science or a vilifier of the human race, depending on one's feeling about evolution. He was seldom looked upon simply as a scientist whose work deserved serious examination, the acceptance or rejection of which should rest upon the scientific validity of the theories it contained. Except for scientists, one accepted or rejected Darwin because of one's previous convictions, not because of the evidence he presented in the *Origin,* and Darwin's defenders were usually every bit as absurd and naïve as were his opponents. Huxley is typical of these younger materialists who found Darwin justifying their beliefs and their prejudices. He therefore promised to sharpen up his "claws and beak" for the coming fray, and from his pen poured forth such statements as: "The publication of the *Origin of Species* marks the Hegira of Science from the idolatries of special creation to the purer faith of Evolution."

The same Thomas Huxley summed up Darwin's role in the "great monkey battle" thus: "He found a great truth trodden underfoot, reviled by bigots, and ridiculed by all the world; he lived long enough to see it, chiefly by his own efforts, irrefragably established in science, inseparably incorporated with the common thoughts of men, and only hated and feared by those who would revile, but dare not." It is difficult to gather more inaccuracies into one complex sentence than Huxley did in the above statement. There was no simple line-up of honest scientists against bigots, as Huxley maintained. There were bigots on both sides, and there were as many capable, honest scientists opposed to Darwin's theory as there were in favor of it. As a matter of fact, only a minority of naturalists, the younger generation to whom Darwin appealed, accepted the *Origin's* central idea.

What actually happened in 1859 when Darwin's work burst upon the world? To begin with, two weeks before publication, on November 11, Darwin had advance copies sent to such noted scientists as Gray, Agassiz, Henslow, and Sedgwick. To each he wrote a note inviting criticism and reaction and hoping for support. Three days before the book was put on sale the well known botanist Watson wrote to Darwin that "Your leading idea will assuredly become recognized as an established truth in science—that is, Natural Selection." The day after publication Huxley sent a highly eulogistic note to Darwin, and within a few days he received another from the preacher and novelist Kingsley. By December 3 he had received many encouraging letters and could write: "We are now a good and compact body of really good men, and in the long run we shall conquer."

But the weight of numbers at first was against Darwin. The Harvard naturalist Agassiz objected that Darwin had not proved his thesis, Gray of the British Museum condemned the book, the Cambridge philosopher Whewell would not allow it in the library of his college, the geologist Lyell refused to put man into Darwin's scheme of evolution, and Adam Sedgwick, professor of geology at Cambridge, considered it an irreligious and immoral book that would destroy faith in the Bible and turn men and women into mere brutes. The first review, which appeared in the *Athanaeum* five days before publication, attacked the theory that man comes from monkeys. The influential *Quarterly Review* condemned the book because it "contradicted the revealed relation of the creature to his Creator" and was "inconsistent with the fullness of His glory." The *Saturday Review* published an antagonistic review on December 24, and two days later the *Daily News* attacked it.

Fortunately for Darwin, Thomas Huxley was asked to do a review for the *Times*. In his lengthy article he went all-out in praise of the *Origin of Species,* and he took it upon himself to write eulogistic articles for the new *Macmillan's Magazine* and the influential *Westminster Review.* Similarly, Dr. Carpenter wrote favorably of Darwin's new book in the *National Review* and the more specialized *Medico-Chirurgical Review.* Thus sides were drawn up by the end of the year for the "great monkey battle," which soon got out of hand. When the British Association for the Advancement of Science met at Oxford in the following summer, Darwin's book was the principal topic of conversation outside the formal sessions. Huxley and Bishop Samuel Wilberforce held an historic debate on the topic in which both wandered far from the point at issue, as when the Anglican Bishop asked Huxley on which side of his family he was descended from the apes, and Huxley answered that at least he had progressed from the primate stage. Both remarks provoked cheers and much waving of handkerchiefs by ladies interested in things "intellectual."

More sensible men realized that the problem was how large a role natural selection was to play in causing variations. Many scientists were willing to allow it an important role, but they insisted that other factors played some part in the evolution of species. Some insisted that use and disuse had been neglected, as Darwin's emendations in later editions tacitly admitted. Others, like the American Asa Gray, wanted to substitute a supernatural selection for Darwin's natural selection. Still others, like Lyell, were willing to admit natural selection's dominant role in causing the origin of new animal species, but they refused to merge man into the evolutionary process—a point on which Darwin remained adamant. Others like Mivart in the *Tablet*, considered Darwin's explanation satisfactory if he would admit a special act of creation by God for man.

There were still others who were willing to concede almost everything Darwin had said, as long as it was not assumed that his theory contained the whole truth. Carlyle summed up this view by remarking caustically: "That the weak and incompetent pass away, while the strong and adequate prevail and continue, appears true enough in animal and human history; but there are mysteries in human life, and in the universe, not explained by that discovery."

Adam Sedgwick, Darwin's former professor, saw the crux of the problem when he accused him of absolute materialism and of falling before the temptation of becoming philosopher and theologian as well as scientist, of jumping unscientifically to conclusions unwarranted by empirically ascertained evidence.

We all admit development as a fact of history [he wrote to Darwin] but how came it about? Here, in language, and still more in logic, we are point-blank at the issue. There is a moral or metaphysical part of nature as well as a physical. A man who denies this is deep in the mire of folly. 'Tis the crown and glory of organic science that it *does*, through *final cause*, link material and moral; and yet *does not* allow us to mingle them in our first conception of laws, and our classification of such laws, whether we consider one side of nature or the other. You have ignored this link; and, if I do not mistake your meaning, you have done your best in one or two pregnant cases to break it. Were it possible (which, thank God, it is not) to break it, humanity, in my mind, would suffer a damage that might brutalize it, and sink the human race into a lower grade of degradation than any into which it has fallen since its written records tell us of its history.

Sedgwick was a grimly accurate prophet, as two world wars have testified, but Darwin could not understand what his former professor was saying.

John Stuart Mill—as objective a seeker after truth as England ever knew—summed up the *Origin's* rightful place in the history of ideas by his comment that although Darwin could not "be said to have proved the truth of his doctrine, he does seem to have proved that it *may* be true, which I take to be as great a triumph as knowledge and ingenuity could possibly achieve on such a question." That seems to be the status of the question today. Much speculation by naturalists since Darwin's day has failed to establish beyond doubt the mechanism whereby evolution works. The evidence in favor of natural selection remains negative rather than positive. It still may be true, as Mill observed, but it has not been proved true, despite Huxley's naïve assertions to the contrary. Later biologists have illuminated the problem, but at the same time they have complicated it. There is no aspect of evolution which is not honestly held in question by contemporary biologists, from natural selection and sexual selection to the causes of variation, the inheritance of acquired characteristics, and the influence of environment.

What about evolution, then, a century after Darwin's great book? For several years he tried to talk some competent scientist into doing a book on man's place in evolution. Lyell refused, and so too did Wallace, even though Darwin offered to turn all his notes over to him. Finally, Darwin was forced to write the book himself, and *The Descent of Man* appeared in 1871. In it Darwin sought to explain "how far the general conclusions arrived at in my former works were applicable to man. . . . The sole object of this work is to consider, firstly, whether man, like every other species, is descended from some pre-existing form; secondly, the manner of his development; and thirdly, the value of the differences between the so-called races of man." In this work Darwin presented evidence purporting to show that the difference between man and beast is only one of degree, that such things as conscience and the moral instinct are the natural product of living together in society. No new ideas either on man or on evolution are to be found in its many pages. It is only an application of the *Origin's* theories to man's evolution from lower forms of life.

In the years since Darwin died, naturalists have accumulated a huge amount of information with which to fill in and modify his work. Even while he was writing the *Origin* an obscure Austrian monk was experimenting with sweet peas to establish laws of heredity and the science of genetics. He published his results in a German journal before Darwin published his *Descent of Man,* but it was not until 1900 that Mendel's work was "discovered." Genetics is used today to explain both likenesses and change from parent to offspring.

Darwin's principle of natural selection has not been discarded, but it has had to make room for other factors, such as use and disuse and the influence of environment. Additional geological discoveries and developments in paleontology in the last century have given naturalists much data on the temporal relationship of various organisms, depending on their place in strata composing the earth's crust. Naturalists today, then, have more evidence in terms of time, mutations, the influence of environment, and the role of natural selection than Darwin had a century ago. They are less dogmatic than he in answering the puzzle of how evolution came about and what part each factor plays in the story of change. The evidence seems to point conclusively to evolution in organic nature, but it still is insufficient to enable naturalists to produce a satisfactory formula—or perhaps it is too much, for on much less evidence Darwin felt justified in producing the formula which is the title of his famous book.

Millions of words have been wasted in the "struggle" between religion and science since the publication of Darwin's *Origin*. The struggle was on false issues, for most people seemed to believe that evolution and religion could not co-exist. One or the other must perish, as the "fitter" survived. This misunderstanding came about partly because the best known proponents of Darwin's theory were materialists like Huxley and Haeckel, men who were happy to use it as a weapon against religion. There were also some religious leaders who believed that the very idea of evolution was irreligious, immoral, and blasphemous. These were the men who made the most noise in the "great monkey battle" and appealed to the simple people whose knowledge of both religion and science was quite unsophisticated.

From the very beginning there were theologians in the Catholic and other churches who realized that any scientifically sound theory of evolution which did not deny God's direct creation of the soul was theologically acceptable. Such men maintained a proper reserve, and did not try to pontificate on scientific findings and theories about which they had no more than amateur knowledge. Generally speaking, the only Christians who could not reconcile their theology and some form of evolution were the Fundamentalists, who believed that every word in the Bible must be accepted in an absolutely literal sense.

Similarly, the only evolutionists who had to give up religion because of science were those who pontificated about ultimates, and thus went, in unscientific fashion, far beyond their factual evidence.

The official stand of the Catholic Church avoided the extremes of either condemning or endorsing each new statement about evolution. Decrees issued by the Pontifical Biblical Commission in 1909 approached the question of evolution obliquely by granting the importance of literary form in interpreting the Bible, and listing truths historically depicted in Genesis, such as the fall of man and his previous creation by God. Most Catholic theologians today seem to believe that naturalists have presented us with sufficient evidence to have established the fact of some kind of evolution. They reject purely materialistic explanations, of course, but otherwise leave the question of how evolution occurred to the naturalists.

More recently many Catholic theologians have been showing that evolution is more compatible with basic theological principles and our knowledge of God's operations than is the older idea of the separate creation of each species by divine intervention in history. Some Catholic theologians and naturalists, such as the recently deceased French Jesuit, Pierre Teilhard de Chardin of France, seem almost to steal

Darwin's thought that "there is grandeur in this view" by showing how the majesty and glory of God can be served only if evolution were a basic fact of history.

The pages of Darwin's book overflowed its covers and flooded the waters of his Idea into almost every area of thought and endeavor since 1859. Darwin had said that through the process of natural selection the fittest survive. But within a short time he was popularly understood to hold that the best survive—which was in perfect accord with the faith people of the nineteenth century put in Progress. There was some basis in Darwin's book for this piece of intellectual sleight of hand, for he believed deep in his heart that, by and large, the fittest were the best, that evolution was synonymous with progress. In his notebook he had written: "From death, famine, rapine, and the concealed war of nature we can see that the highest good which we can conceive, the creation of the highest animals, has directly come." The same idea is expressed in almost the same words in the poetic last paragraph of the *Origin*. Darwin had said fittest, but he confused fittest with best in his own mind, and occasionally the confusion showed up in his writing.

Natural selection was therefore understandably taken as the mechanism whereby this Progress, so evident even to the casual observer of 1859, actually took place. It was comforting to think that the human race was driving inevitably to perfection, that the weaker, more corrupt members fell by the wayside, that the struggle for existence was a great screening process whereby the best specimens, physically and morally, were sifted by natural selection and allowed to propagate their kind. All this was done mechanically by self-sufficient laws of nature; a cosmic purpose had replaced a divine purpose, and, as Darwin's wife commented ruefully on her husband's work, it put God "further off."

That is why the *Origin* must be included among the world's important books even though contingent circumstances rather than its own merit made it of such great consequence. One of Darwin's best biographers, Geoffrey West, sums up its impact on the Western mind by saying: "The effect was truly tremendous. Almost by the mere statement of a new principle of approach, dynamic, not static, he revolutionized every department of study, from astronomy to history, from paleontology to psychology, from embryology to religion." Darwin seemed to redeem the nineteenth century from chaos out of which earlier static thought could bring no order. He apparently explained the mystery of life and the process of progress. His was a Master Idea of the century.

This Master Idea appealed to all kinds of people: it used the concept of matter and motion to explain life itself; in evolution it offered a method for tracing the origin of all things, and people thought that exhaustively tracing something to its origin completely explained it; it offered a pragmatic test of value, survival, which could be applied to insects or to human institutions; it made the highly competitive economic system of the next century a natural thing following the eternal law of struggle for existence and survival of the fittest; it explained the "miracle of Progress," and it promised untold Progress in the future. It was an unconscious rationalization and justification by a respectable scientist of the temper of his age. Fighting was the order of the day, in business, in diplomacy, in war; and Darwin had explained scientifically how from struggle the highest good emerges, how, from struggle and through the survival of the fittest lowly animals, majestic man had originated. This was the right tune played in the right key in 1859 and for decades afterwards.

So the age snatched up Darwin's Master Idea and applied it to all fields of thought. It was used to give scientific credentials to what the age had been doing for some time, and by so doing it both justified and promoted these trends. The Master Idea was a three-sided idea consisting of struggle for existence in which the fittest survive through the process of natural selection. This was taken to mean that morality was outmoded, as Sedgwick had complained, and as a Manchester reviewer observed when he said that according to the *Origin of Species* "might is right and therefore Napoleon is right and every cheating tradesman is also right."

This popular application of Darwin's three-sided Master Idea was not always fair to Darwin, but he fathered the idea and could not logically deny his paternity of the popularized offspring that came to be known as Social Darwinism. In the last chapter of the *Origin* he suggested that his theories be applied to such subjects as geology and psychology, that by its application to social studies "much light will be thrown on the origin of man and his history."

The idea of struggle being a natural and a good thing permeated the book. Darwin approved of this struggle because of the beneficent results which came from it; it was for this reason, and not for any moral scruples, that he refused to contribute to the defense of Bradlaugh for circulating a book on birth control. He wrote in answer to a request for money that he "disagreed with preventive checks to population on the ground that over-multiplication was useful, since it caused a struggle for existence in which only the strongest and ablest survived." And the fittest, those who win the wars or make the most money, are hailed as the best. In the closing pages of the *Origin* Darwin observed: "As natural selection works solely by and for the good of each being, all corporeal and mental endowments will tend to progress towards perfection." It is for this reason that West concludes: "Popular Darwinism may be a crude but it is scarcely an unfair or inaccurate presentation of the broad effect of Darwin's basic writings."

Darwinism was used to explain everything from language to war and religion. Bishop Trench, an Anglican language authority, showed how the fittest words survive and the less fit become obsolete. Sir Henry Maine, an authority on government, wrote of the "beneficent private war which makes one man strive to climb on the shoulders of another and remain there through the law of the survival of fittest." Darwinism was used to justify competition with no holds barred as a natural struggle for existence among business firms. The fittest survived, and the world progressed as weak—or honest—firms went bankrupt and were eliminated from the struggle.

So it was with human beings. Eugenists, like Sir Francis Galton, were convinced Darwinists, who consciously applied his theories to society to conclude that since men are not equal and since inequalities are inherited, social misfits should be allowed to perish and should be prevented from breeding additional inferior stock. Herbert Spencer invoked Darwin to show how, "under the natural order of things, society is constantly excreting its unhealthy, imbecile, slow, vacillating, faithless members."

The idea was applied to social groups by such men as Walter Bagehot and Ludwig Gumplowicz—and the path led straight from them to Mussolini and Hitler. Bagehot taught that "social progress took place only because the struggle for existence caused men to form strong, compact social groups having despotic control over the entire conduct of their members." History is the record of the struggle between groups, and in time between national groups. Those groups which are most tightly organized, most compact and homogeneous, are victorious. So Bagehot concludes: "What you want is a comprehensive rule binding men together, making them do much the same things . . . fashioning them alike, and keeping them so."

Others picked up the Darwinian idea of struggle

for existence and survival of the fittest to apply it to races. Thus the Nazi Alfred Rosenberg follows Darwin in writing that history is the "dramatic battle of distinct races," that survival is the only test of value between races, that the struggle is inevitable and perpetual. In the same way, Darwin's idea was used to justify war as a form of struggle between nations from which good is bound to come. Darwin himself believed that a short war benefits the world because it brings out good social qualities without killing off too many fit men. Bagehot approved of war because "the hard impact of military virtues beats meanness out of the world," and Spencer insisted that "without war, the world would still have been inhabited only by men of feeble types sheltering in caves and living on wild food."

Whether he realized it or not, Darwin had sanctified struggle as history's great selector and purifier which promised untold blessings in the future. One individual who had written eleven years earlier that "The history of all hitherto existing society is the history of class struggles," hailed the *Origin of Species* as a scientific counterpart and justification of what he was doing in the social sciences. This was Karl Marx, who earlier in 1859 had published his *Critique of Political Economy.*

Chapter II

A Century of Marxian Communism

In January, 1859, Marx wrote the preface to his *Critique of Political Economy* and sent the manuscript to a publisher. In this preface he penned what is probably the most pregnant paragraph of the last century, a paragraph that contains the seed of all Marx's basic thought. The preface is an autobiographical account of Marx's studies and research till 1859, and in it he arrives at the conclusion "which continued to serve as the leading thread in my studies":

In the social production which men carry on, they enter into definite relations that are indispensable and independent of their will; these relations of production correspond to a definite stage of development of their material powers of production. The sum total of these relations of production constitutes the economic structure of society—the real foundation, on which rise legal and political superstructures and to which correspond definite forms of social consciousness. The mode of production in material life determines the general character of the social, political and spiritual processes of life. It is not the consciousness of men that determines their existence, but, on the contrary, their social existence determines their consciousness. At a certain stage of their development, the material forces of production in society come in conflict with the existing relations of production, or—what is but a legal expression for the same thing— with the property relations within which they had been at work before. From forms of development of the forces of production, these relations turn into their fetters. Then comes the period of social revolution. . . . Just as our opinion of an individual is not based on what he thinks of himself, so can we not judge of such a period of transformation by its own consciousness; on the contrary, this consciousness must rather be explained from the contradictions of material life, from the existing conflict between the social forces of production and the relations of production. No social order ever disappears before all the productive forces, for which there is room in it, have been developed; and new, higher relations of production never appear before the material conditions of their existence have matured in the womb of the old society. . . . In broad outlines we can designate the Asiatic, the ancient, the feudal, and the modern bourgeois methods of production as so many epochs in the progress of the economic formation of society. The bourgeois relations of production are the last antagonistic form of the social process of production—antagonistic not in the sense of individual antagonism, but of one arising from conditions surrounding the life of individuals in society; at the same time the productive forces developing in the womb of bourgeois society create the material conditions for the solution of that antagonism. This social formation constitutes, therefore, the closing chapter of the prehistoric stage of human society.[1]

There have been many solid analyses of Marx's thought since his death in 1883. Here it is only necessary to point out the most salient features of that thought. But it might be observed beforehand that Marx modified his thinking through the years, and it is possible that he worked his way out of the web of historical materialism he wove in mid-life. For more than half his writings have never been published. His associate Friedrich Engels had a difficult time editing the third volume of *Das Kapital* so as to align it with Marx's earlier volumes, nor did he ever publish Marx's later writings. When Marx's unpublished papers fell into the hands of the Russian communists, they promised to publish them all—but not a line of these has ever been put into print. Shortly after Khrushchev came to power he promised that Marx's unpublished papers would soon appear,

[1] *A Contribution to the Critique of Political Economy* (Chicago: Charles H. Kerr Co., 1904), pp. 11–13.

an enigmatic statement which in 1959 might mean almost anything. But as yet nothing has seen the light of print.

Marx posits an evolutionary world. He admired Darwin and wanted to dedicate *Das Kapital* to him, for he believed that he was doing for social science what Darwin had done for natural science. When Engels pronounced the funeral oration over Marx's grave, he observed: "Just as Darwin discovered the law of evolution in organic nature, so Marx discovered the law of evolution in human history." Marx discovered the law of evolution, however, not in Darwin but in Hegel. This noted German philosopher had explained all history as moving in a certain pattern called "the dialectic." This theory asserts that contradiction is the very essence of reality, that a thing both is and is not at the same time, for it is has no static reality. Reality, according to Hegel, is auto-dynamic. By its very nature it generates a contradiction of itself, following the always-repeated process of going from thesis to antithesis to synthesis.

Marx and Engels claimed that they stood Hegel on his feet to explain all history in terms of the dialectic as applied to the class struggle. At each age in history, they held, the dominant class imposes a system of production-relations on society, which generates a class necessarily antagonistic to the dominant class and sworn to overthrow it. Thus production-relations in medieval society produced a class of serfs and merchants who were unprivileged, were outside society as it were, and fought to overthrow it. And in modern times capitalism produces a proletariat who are exploited by the owners of the means of production and are necessarily committed to over-turning this system of production. Revolution is therefore of the essence of history until the classless society is achieved.

This is why Marx and Engels opened the *Communist Manifesto* with the challenging statement that, "the history of all hitherto existing society is the history of class struggles." The only real class divisions, Marx believed, were economic divisions based on one's relation to the production system of any given age. National, racial, religious, linguistic, and other divisions were artificial in his thought, and that is why he firmly believed that in any future war the proletariat of the world would make common cause against governments' putting them on the sacrificial altar in order to keep the capitalistic system alive.

Class relations, he maintained, are determined by production-relations. This is a point frequently overlooked by analysts of Marxian theory—that the distinctively human thing about man is that he is a producer. Not rationality but means of production distinguishes man from lower animals. "They begin to differentiate themselves from animals," Marx wrote of men, "as soon as they begin to produce their means of subsistence." Thus production is the basic, determining, dominating fact of life. Marx expressed it in these words:

This mode of production must not be considered merely from the aspect that it is the reproduction of the physical existence of individuals. It is rather in fact a definite form of activity of these individuals, a definite mode of life. As individuals express their life, so they are. What they are therefore coincides with their production—what they produce as well as how they produce. What individuals are therefore depends on the material conditions of their production.[2]

A bricklayer therefore prays as a bricklayer, votes as a bricklayer, thinks as a bricklayer, bowls or plays softball as a bricklayer. Similarly, a manufacturer goes to church as a manufacturer, contributes to the

United Fund as a manufacturer, and watches television as a manufacturer.

Marx pictures history as moving on three levels. The first determines the second, and the second the third. The first or bottom level of history is production-relations, which determine class alignments and the mutual antagonism of the classes. For the method of production at any given time is the basic factor of history, according to Marx, and the determinant of all historical events. The second level of history is the class struggle between those who seek to perpetuate the existing order and those who want to overthrow it. The third level or superstructure of history consists of things political, educational, cultural, and so on, "emanations" of the class struggle whereby the dominant class attempts to consolidate itself in power. Thus the school system, religions, museums, operas, and other media forming public opinion are used by capitalists as "opium" to distract the proletariat from the class struggle and to justify bourgeois control of society.

This is the meaning of Marxian materialism—it is not the "vulgar" materialism of such previous thinkers as Holbach or La Mettrie, but a materialism which admits ideals and spiritual drives among men but asserts that they are rationalizations of an economic position. "The ideal," Marx wrote, "is nothing other than the material world reflected by the human mind and translated into forms of thought." Thus Marxists can admit the moving power of religion, movies, music, and popular opinion, but all these are supposed to be determined by the material reality of the class struggle and, underlying this, the production-relations of any given time in history. In our day, Marxists argue, religion, movies, newspapers and other media forming public opinion are instruments used by the producers to keep the proletariat in chains.

Marx's great popularity through the last century, however, rests not so much on his positive doctrine as upon his trenchant criticism of the capitalistic system. His protest appeal was strong because there were glaring abuses in capitalism which were long accepted by all except a few "radicals." Here, of course, Marx is inconsistent, since he insists on a deterministic arrangement of the social order based on production-relations. But his inconsistency did not detract from his appeal. Thus Marxism was given a missionary drive backed by a strong moral sense that injustices against the working class must be eliminated.

Marx also appealed to the working class as the prophet of a better day in the future. He adroitly combined the accouterments of science with the spirit of prophecy, for his work is full of facts and statistics combined with indignant outbursts against abuses in the capitalistic system. He promised that by the necessity of the dialectical process the revolution would come and there could finally be realized the ideal of "from each according to his ability, to each according to his need." There would be an ideal classless society with no form of coercion, no police, no state, no armies or war, and all relationships would be happy and voluntary.

Naïve as Marxism might seem to the critic, it must be realized that it was as irrefutable to one who believed it as his faith is to the Christian. The dialectic is the cardinal mystery in Marxism, and it is used to explain away all contradictions. Attacks on Marxian economics or philosophy of history are dismissed as coming from those who do not think in the dialectic but rather in discredited rationalistic terms. Thus, at least for a time, it was possible for convinced Marxists to believe that the Soviet Union was achieving the stateless society by growing stronger and more tyrannical, that somehow by going right one takes the first step toward the left. Because of the dialectic, it was impossible for Marxists and their critics to meet on common ground—just as a rationalist agnostic and a believing Christian cannot find common ground for discussing miracles or the divinity of Christ.

There was considerable truth in Marx's critique of capitalistic society, as Christians and capitalists have admitted explicitly or implicitly in their reforming of this society. But the critique was essentially wrong. It was atheistic and materialistic. Its morality was that of the class struggle. All these are basic errors, any one of which vitiates the whole system. The weakness of Marx's analysis of capitalism, however, has shown up in the last century chiefly in the view he took of man as a robot whose every reaction is determined by his place in the productive process. Here Marx made the same error that the *laissez-faire* economists made when they postulated an "economic man."

Economic drives count for a great deal in history, but they are only one force among many. Marx has them work out to logical conclusions both in individual men and in society at large. Thus he sees capitalists ruthlessly competing with each other until only one or two are left in each industry. Thus he sees employers paying ever more miserable wages as they themselves grow ever more wealthy. Marx apparently never realized that men do not live by logic alone any more than by bread alone. There is more adaptability in man than Marx ever admitted, and the system he called "capitalism" is more supple than he thought possible.

Since Marx's death in 1883 most industrialists and most employees have co-operated within the so-called capitalistic system to modify it in their common interests, to adjust it so that wealth is better distributed, to regulate it in order to eliminate its worst abuses. Employers and employees will always have their differences, to be sure, but what Marx failed to realize is that these differences can be settled to the common interest of all parties by measures short of class war. The modifications in capitalism, which Marx would have considered inconceivable, have given most workers fairly decent wages and a measure of security unknown even to businessmen in 1859. He would not have been able to conceive of capitalists contributing to such social security programs as unemployment compensation or retirement funds.

Thus in one sense Marx turned out to be a poor prophet. For neither capitalist nor employee has followed the road this last century which Marx drew on the map of history in 1859. This is the unfortunate aspect of making a great discovery, and it has happened many times in history. As Freud resolved all human behavior ultimately into terms of sex, so Marx blinded himself to the complexity of man and social organization by resolving everything ultimately into production-relations and resultant class war. He accorded too much to ruthless competition and not enough to co-operation.

It is impossible to trace the influence of Marx through the century, just as it is impossible to show adequately the influence of St. Augustine or John Calvin through subsequent history. For Marx's thought has had influence on all segments of society in the Western world, and it has spread to China, India, and other places in the Orient as well. It has even had some effect on Christian social thought and papal social encyclicals. We can nevertheless follow official Marxism from the publication of the *Critique of Political Economy* until 1959.

Karl Marx obtained an amplifier through which he shouted to the world when the First International was organized in 1864. Marx was on the platform when trade unionists met in St. Martin's Hall in London to discuss how to check the immigration of workers into England. He was a member of the provisional committee, wrote the inaugural address, and composed the provisional rules. Thus he was able to make the First International the medium through which his doctrine was presented to the working class in Europe.

Dissension broke out as various groups challenged Marx's domination of the First International. With the expulsion of the anarchist Bakunin in 1876, the organization collapsed. Before the Second International was organized in 1889, Marx had died a relatively obscure man. Nevertheless, in the years between the first two Internationals, Socialism enjoyed steady growth in Europe, increasing from about 400,000 voters in 1876 to about a million in 1889. Growth was greatest in Germany, where the Social Democratic Party, persecuted by Bismarck, grew increasingly strong with each election. The working classes in England and the United States did not take to Marxism. In these countries it was supported mainly by European refugees. Nor did it make great headway in the Latin countries, where the more radical anarchism had a greater appeal.

Toward the end of the century, however, Marxism began to make considerable inroads into the Slavic countries.

The Second International was formed at a Congress of Workers held in Paris on the centenary of the French Revolution in 1889. It lasted exactly twenty-five years, coming to an abrupt end with the beginning of the first World War. The Second International claimed Marx as its intellectual guide and looked upon itself as the means of spreading Marxism and promoting the revolution of the proletariat. But there was no general agreement on "what Marx really meant." Four principal schools of exegesis developed on the meaning of Marxism. An evolutionary school held that the revolution could not occur until capitalism had reached a certain stage of development, until it became ripe, as it were, and ready to fall from the tree of time. A revisionist school held that communists should work within the democratic party system until they had a clear preponderance of support, and then by legal steps they should revise the regime to put productive property under social control and to create the classless society. A syndicalist school held that communists should aim at immediate, violent revolution. When the dust of the class struggle settled, they held, it would be time enough to think of the future society. Finally, the Bolshevik school, dominated by Lenin, held for violent revolution under the control of a highly disciplined, tightly controlled party, "the vanguard of the proletariat," who were to rule in the interim between the revolution and the realization of the final communist state.

The first World War had profound effects on the development of Marxism. With few exceptions, Marxists in all countries joined in the war effort, voting their governments war credits, and volunteering or submitting to the draft. Thus was exploded Marx's faith that, when once properly educated, the proletariat would refuse to participate in international wars but would join hands in rising against their perpetrators. Several million men had been exposed to the Marxian "truth," and still went out to kill their fellow workers in other lands. Intelligent people saw that nationalism made a stronger appeal to the masses of men than did Marxism.

In a second way did the first World War profoundly affect Marxism. It occasioned the collapse of the tsarist regime in Russia, and in little more than half a year the Bolsheviks were in power. For a time they had to struggle for their lives against the Russian White Army and the intervention of Allied troops. But within a few years they consolidated themselves in power, apparently with fairly general popular support, and were ready to begin the great experiment of putting communism into practice.

For three years the Soviet Union floundered under "pure communism," as workers tried to run factories and peasants expropriated the land. Production fell off alarmingly, there was want and hunger throughout the country, and people began to cry "Down with the Soviets!" Whereupon Lenin pragmatically reverted to capitalistic devices to increase production. Most factories were returned to private ownership, piece work was reintroduced, differential wages paid, and peasants allowed to operate their own farms.

Lenin and his successor Stalin always professed allegiance to Marxian theory. But they never let it get in their way. When Lenin died in 1924, the Bolsheviks were solidly in power in the U.S.S.R., but communism was almost as far off as ever. In the struggle for power after Lenin's death, Stalin emerged successfully over Trotsky. The latter was a literal Marxist who believed in promoting world-wide revolution at once, whereas Stalin held that the U.S.S.R. must first be strengthened as the bastion of communism in a hostile capitalist world. In a certain profound sense, Stalin's victory over Trotsky was a defeat for Marxism.

Although Stalin never officially repudiated Marxian doctrine, under him the practical drift was in the direction of Russian nationalism. There was more talk about distinctive Russian characteristics, the "Internationale" was replaced with a patriotic national anthem, and Bolshevik foreign policy followed the pattern set down by the tsars since the time of Peter the Great. These things could be done while Stalin remained "loyal" to Marxism because of new standards of truth which are absolutely incomprehensible to men in the Western tradition. When Stalin insisted there can be no relation between words and deeds, this is exactly what he meant.

What, then, happened to Marxism under Stalin and his successors? It continued to be preached against the capitalistic world, but it was not followed in the Soviet Union. For those relatively intelligent persons who were taken in by Marxian doctrine, the Soviet experiment was disillusioning. No longer could the ideal classless society be held forth as an El Dorado on the horizon. The communist society had been realized and it meant the tyranny of a few over the masses. It meant regimentation and exploitation such as capitalism never accomplished. Fetters that were supposed to be loosed were screwed tighter. The state that was to melt away grew continually stronger and more repressive. Promised freedoms were never realized.

The Soviet experiment therefore ended the promise of Marxian communism for most people in the Western world. A few dreamers continued to think it possible under different conditions, and a few unscrupulous politicians used it as a means of achieving personal power. But for the masses it had lost its appeal.

Meanwhile, the official guardian of Marxism was the Third International or the Comintern, with headquarters in Moscow and dominated by Soviet members. Through the Comintern, communists in countries throughout the world were directed in their struggle against "capitalism." But Marxism was clearly subordinated to the interests of the U.S.S.R. as the Comintern was utilized to promote Soviet foreign policy. Thus communists were ordered to be friendly with democracies when the "Popular Front" was promoted in 1935, and again to call off their attacks on Hitler when the Soviet Union and Germany entered into a pact in 1939.

In recent years the light of Marxian thought has burned more brightly in the Orient than in the Western world. But nowhere today except in a few theoreticians' minds and in books is there anything like pure Marxism. What is called "communism" is the doctrine of Marx as strained through the Soviet experiment and applied to such countries as Red China and the European nations behind the Iron Curtain. In these places Marxian doctrine seems a hollow mockery invoked from time to time because of its strong protest appeal against the economic and social system of the Western world.

The reality in these countries is something from which Karl Marx would likely have turned with indignation. For it is the reality of a small group ruthlessly holding power over millions of little people whose thought and emotions they control with almost diabolical cleverness. What these leaders actually think and believe we of the Western world do not know, for there is no correspondence between their words and what they profess to believe. Perhaps they believe that ultimately they will realize Marx's goal of the classless society of perfectly free men. Perhaps they have completely abandoned that goal. Whatever they believe, however, we can be sure that their beliefs will never interfere with their struggle to maintain power and to defeat the Western world they consider their sworn enemy.

In a sense, then, Marxism is dead in 1959. But in the century since the publication of Marx's *Critique of Political Economy* it has played a decisive role in what the future may see as the greatest revolution of all time—a revolution which coincides with an age of imperialism and the revolt of the rest of the world against Western, Christian civilization.

Chapter III

A Century of Concern Over Personal Freedoms

JOHN STUART MILL was a remarkable man. Without benefit of formal schooling he became one of the most influential thinkers in the nineteenth century. He was educated by his extremely severe father, being introduced to classical and contemporary works, which he was taught to dissect at an early age. He read Aristotle in Greek at the age of five. Used as an educational experiment by his father and the latter's utilitarian associates, he never knew the games or pleasures of childhood. His mind was developed as though he were an angel instead of a human being. Small wonder, then, that he was overwhelmed by the first emotional poetry he read, that he had a youthful nervous breakdown, and that he gave himself so completely to Mrs. Harriet Taylor, whom he loved at a distance for twenty years and then married after Mr. Taylor died and Mill was forty-five.

With his beloved wife—to whom he attributed

all imaginable virtue and intelligence—he worked on a number of publications. The most important of these was *On Liberty*, which was still not published when she died late in 1858. Early in 1859, he published this classic defense of liberty as a memorial to her and as a precious memory to him of her close collaboration in his works. "After my irreparable loss," he tells us in his *Autobiography*, "one of my earliest cares was to print and publish the treatise, so much of which was the work of her whom I had lost, and consecrate it to her memory. I have made no alteration or addition to it, nor shall I ever."

On Liberty is a classic defense of personal freedoms that retains its cogency after a century. John Stuart Mill observed in his *Autobiography* that it was likely to survive longer than his other works because the conditions prompting it were growing worse, and there was no reason to expect them to get better in the future. Mill published the book with a dedication that, one of his contemporaries remarked, would have killed a lesser man's work with ridicule. The dedication read, in part:

To the beloved and deplored memory of her who was the inspirer, and in part the author, of all that is best in my writings—the friend and wife whose exalted sense of truth and right was my strongest incitement, and whose approbation was my chief reward—I dedicate this volume. . . . Were I but capable of interpreting to the world one-half the great thoughts and noble feelings which are buried in her grave, I should be the medium of a greater benefit to it than is ever likely to arise from anything that I can write, unprompted and unassisted by her all but unrivaled wisdom.

In this work, Mill is not concerned with freedom of the will, but rather with the absence of restraint on an individual to think and act as he likes. In other words, what are "the nature and limits of the power which can be legitimately exercised by society over the individual?" He was concerned with the way society tries to make all individuals conform to the same line of thought, with the propensity of many well-intentioned persons to suggest legislation suppressing dissent, and thus "to impose their own opinions and inclinations as a rule of conduct on others." This tendency was increasing, Mill feared, and therefore he felt compelled to erect "a strong barrier of moral conviction" against it.

Mill's argument is basically weak. But it is logically constructed and intellectually compelling when once its utilitarian presuppositions are accepted. He argues that society has no right to interfere with an individual's thought or expression. It may interfere with his action only for its own self-protection. It may therefore control only those acts which have social consequence. To put the matter concretely: society would have no right to prohibit a man from getting drunk if he stayed in his room until he was perfectly sober; but it would have a right to punish him for getting drunk if this caused him to become violent and to endanger other people's life or property. A century after Mill wrote it is difficult to imagine any kind of thought or action which does not have at least remote social consequences. The drunk who sobers up in his room robs society of his services; a young man's sleeping in the classroom, which seems to hurt no one but himself, may be robbing society of a potentially great engineer. Thus Mill's distinction seems to break down to a matter of degree rather than of kind.

Mill had additional reasons for advocating full freedom of thought and expression to all, substantial reasons which bear careful attention today. First, a suppressed opinion may be true. To deny such a possibility is to assume infallibility for the majority or for the government. Second, even though erroneous, the opinion may contain an element of truth which can be incorporated by society only if its proponents are allowed freely to argue for it. Third, even if the suppressed opinion be totally wrong, the truth is better developed and more fully understood if it has to defend itself rather than prevail by silencing all opposition.

As regards freedom of action, Mill intuitively felt that a society in which all people conformed to exactly the same standards was somehow a deadening environment for human development. He concedes that society has the right to control the individual's actions as a matter of self-protection. But the great proportion of what we do has direct consequences only on ourselves. *On Liberty* is replete with assertions which come from Mill's sensitivity rather than from reasoned argument. "At present individuals are lost in the crowd." "That so few now dare to be eccentric, marks the chief danger of the time." "There is no reason that all human existence should be constructed on some one, or some small number of patterns." "Society has now fairly got the better of individuality; and the danger which threatens human nature is not the excess, but the deficiency, of personal impulses and preferences."

These and many other remarks from *On Liberty* could easily be attributed to any elderly individualistic professor in 1959. For how many in our day dare be different? Why must both shoes be black? or brown? Why, at a given time in a given locality, must all people have the same opinions and say the same things? Social conformity was a serious matter to Mill because he believed that it depressed society and prevented progress. When all poets have identical feelings and express them in similar phrases, poetry is decadent. When every businessman follows the same formula, there is no change and no progress. When all citizens mouth the same opinions, political life is dead.

Mill was apparently wrong in tying individuality and progress so closely together, for progress has increased while individuality has receded in the last hundred years. But there is another point he raised which should cause us concern. "Genius," he asserted, "can only breathe freely in an *atmosphere* of freedom." No one can say how much genius has been smothered in the past century by social conformity; but a quick inventory of those who might be considered geniuses suggests that they were nonconformists. The use of authority in the classroom or the business enterprise to obtain conformity violates in a subtle way the individual's right to be himself. Business companies that designate the kind of car, the cut of suit, the type of home that junior executives must have each season violate Mill's norms of liberty. They also infringe on their employees' individual rights.

Mill's views on liberty changed somewhat in later life. They were published posthumously in a work significantly entitled *On Social Freedom*. Here Mill is less concerned with "the dead hand of government" than with social limitations on freedom. Moreover, in his later work he is no longer the complete individualist, for he sees that "association, not isolation, of interests is the school in which excellencies are nurtured." *On Social Freedom* analyzes freedom as a matter of choice, maintaining that the free choice is that prompted by the highest of motives. Mill concludes: "We meet with the notion that the main limitations upon men's freedom are owing to oppressive or unjust laws, enforced by civil governments. I believe most firmly that this is a fallacy which is as mischievous as it is absurd."

Man destroys his own freedom by acting impulsively, from base motives, or through mere habit. Social restraints on freedom include such things as desire for pecuniary gain, fear of losing respect or good will, fear of social ostracism, of ridicule, or someone's opinion, and mere social etiquette. Mill concludes on a somber note:

There is a vast, vague, mysterious authority which casts its shadow over all human affairs, and which governs men's actions with a far more stringent rule than that exercised by the civil governor—the authority of Conventionalism or Conventional Propriety. There is a strange and vague dread of doing what no one else ever does, of being altogether singular, which more frequently restrains men—excepting the lowest or poorest classes in society, and perhaps *not* excepting these— from the indulgence of their personal fancies and caprices, than the prohibitions of civil law.

The past century has been rather careless of Mill's prophecies about liberty. It has proved him right about the increasing desire to conform and about decreasing individualism, but it has proved him generally wrong about governments no longer being a danger to liberty. Some governments stoutly resisted the frenetic demands of some people to restrict liberty in the name of security and conformity. These were especially governments in the Anglo-Saxon tradition, whose peoples had purchased liberty at a steep price in medieval and early modern times and who were less concerned with philosophical definition of the concept than with hedging it in securely with constitutional, legislative, and procedural guarantees.

As a rule, freedoms were established in the Anglo-Saxon tradition first in England, and then passed on as part of the "rights of Englishmen" to countries such as the United States and Australia. An Englishman was once executed for "imagining" treason; several times others were executed on the word of a single individual who later turned out to be a false witness. Some were legislated to death by "bills of attainder" when no law could be found under which to prosecute them. These and other concrete violations of a person's liberty caused Englishmen to define treason and to work out through the centuries the "due process of law" by which men may be arrested, tried, and convicted.

By 1859, these procedures were so firmly established that they could resist tempestuous times. In this country there were occasional flagrant violations of personal liberties, as during the Civil War, in the frenzy of fear about things "un-American" after the first World War, and in the years after the second World War. Most frequently, these campaigns to restrict liberty have been conducted by individuals and groups, with the government tending to ignore or resist them. In the century since 1859, the United States Supreme Court has developed the doctrine that freedom of expression and of association may be denied only if its purpose is illegal or if it will lead to immediate violence. Many intelligent people question whether, under existing conditions in the divided world of 1959, such a doctrine does not invite disaster. And equally intelligent persons point out that there is no point to our destroying the very liberties we claim we are trying to preserve.

Even in Anglo-Saxon countries conditions have made it necessary for governments to close in more tightly on personal liberties. Back in 1859, men like John Bright insisted it was a violation of their personal freedom for a government to protect employees by legislation on working conditions; that it was a violation of freedom of contract for a government to set minimum wages or maximum hours for workers. But these and many other violations—if they be violations—of personal freedom have become part of the law of every land. Businessmen operate under a thousand or more laws which restrict them in a thousand or more ways. Speed limits and "no parking" signs prevail in every congested area. When people are packed together, their freedoms are necessarily curtailed. You can shout "Fire!" in the middle of a desert without harm, but not in a packed auditorium. And the world has been growing more and more like a packed auditorium since 1859.

No sensible person feels that personal liberty is endangered by these necessary regulations. This is a contrast from half a century ago, when some people argued that it was a personal injustice for the government to pass a pure food and drug act to protect consumers from unscrupulous merchants. In a sense, then, governments have had to restrict formerly unrestrained liberties in order to preserve a society in which basic freedoms can prevail.

In countries outside the Anglo-Saxon tradition, liberty has lived more precariously this last century. Generally speaking, it has been championed by minorities and treated cavalierly by majorities. Personal liberty has been highly prized in the Latin countries since 1859, as it was before, but it has been severely restricted by governments from time to time in all these countries. Napoleon III found it necessary, beginning in 1859, to make concessions to the Liberals, but he still maintained arbitrary censorship over the press, and by various restrictive laws kept the French Liberals in exile until his fall in 1870. In the name of liberty the French Third Republic pursued various illiberal policies, such as its attack on the Church early in this century.

Latin peoples failed to strike an equilibrium between personal liberty and despotic rule. Everyone enshrined liberty as an ideal, but for them it meant individual license for themselves and silence or prison for their opponents. One cannot say that liberty has either made progress or lost ground in the Latin countries in the last century. In Spain it never took secure root, though it was never lost as an ideal. As soon as such a Liberal as Azaña came to power in the Spanish Revolution he had passed a law giving him dictatorial power and making a mockery of personal freedoms. And today under Franco freedom has gone underground.

In France personal liberty refuses to die or even to grow weak. Despite any legislation to the contrary, liberty burns strong in most Frenchmen's hearts because they are attached to the French Revolution and its triad of *liberté, égalité, fraternité*. In Italy, liberty has survived Mussolini, and personal freedoms seem on a more solid foundation in 1959 than they were a century before, when Cavour set about unifying the Italian states. In the Latin American countries, liberty has survived countless crises and the general trend toward caudillism or personal rule. Perón ended a failure in Argentina, as many similar figures were in the various Latin American states before him. And in the name of liberty and personal freedom insurgents came out of the hills of Cuba in 1959 to overthrow Batista—just a century after Mill published *On Liberty*.

Liberty may not always shine brightly in the Latin countries, but it is a flame which has never gone out in the last century and, at least in the Latin American countries, it has burned more consistently and more brightly.

Not so in the Slavic countries. Etymologically, there is antithesis between the words "liberty" or freedom and "Slavic" or slave. But the Slavic peoples, who sometimes seem condemned to a tragic existence, have made a number of heroic bids for liberty since 1859. In 1863, the Poles made a desperate attempt to obtain freedom from the Russian tsar. Unsupported by Western Europe, they were crushed. Similar bids have periodically been made since then, sometimes successfully, as by the Rumanians and the Poles later on, sometimes unsuccessfully, as by the Hungarians in 1956.

Liberty for the Slavic peoples seems to be conceived in national or tribal terms rather than individual. From 1859 until today, various Slavic groups have agitated for national freedom or independence —and in the last century some of them won it, most of them to lose it again as they rushed quickly to personal rule or dictatorship and showed little understanding of what Mill meant by freedom when he published his famous essay in 1859. Nevertheless, a sound feeling for liberty remains alive in the hearts of Hungarians and Slavic peoples behind the Iron Curtain who heroically keep alive the desire for personal freedom in a land where everything is cleverly arranged to make it easy and agreeable to conform.

There was an inkling of profound truth behind Mill's observation in 1859 that social conformity was a greater danger to liberty than governmental coercion. For liberty cannot be killed by force. Coercion only nourishes it. But it can be smothered—die in its sleep as it were—by not being exercised daily. John Stuart Mill's fear of the "vast, vague, mysterious authority . . . of Conventionalism" was well placed in 1859. A century later it is even better placed, for "conventionalism" has acquired the big guns of newspaper chains, radio, movies, television, and mass advertising.

Older people in 1959 contrast their "active" lives as young people with that of their children and grandchildren who watch baseball and football games instead of playing on the corner lot. There is also much talk about the way that "disc jockeys" dictate how teen-agers are to think, feel, and act. Although there is truth in these observations, it is difficult to determine how much freedom has been surrendered by the masses of people and how much they desire to be exactly like everyone else. It is hard to tell to what extent ladies and gentlemen followed the dictates of fashion in 1859, for in that time fashions did not change annually and everyone dressed pretty much as his parents had done and were doing. But there is no doubt that, although people possess and occasionally exercise personal freedom, in most aspects of daily living they are content to follow the dictates of advertisers and columnists and experts in newspapers and magazines and on radio and television.

In 1959, a century after John Stuart Mill published his defense of liberty and his warning about its future, there is reason to ask whether the generality of mankind want fredom. This seems a startling question to people in the Anglo-Saxon tradition, but the ease with which dictators assumed power in most of the world in the last century suggests that most people prefer to surrender their freedom for food and security. Even people in the Anglo-Saxon countries may not prize liberty as greatly as they think. For liberty is a "package deal." A people can preserve it only by accepting its accompanying responsibilities and burdens. There are times, indeed, when liberty seems more a burden than a gift, for it entails more than freedom to express one's self. It entails freedom of decision. One who prizes freedom and accepts its responsibilities must make up his own mind on questions of public policy after examining all available relative evidence and arguments. There are times, then, when liberty must seem to those who understand it almost like the albatross hanging on the neck of the Ancient Mariner.

Whether men want freedom is the question underlying Ivan's "Legend of the Grand Inquisitor," the sketch of a proposed novel he relates to Alyosha in *The Brothers Karamazov*. Ivan has Christ return to earth, this time in Spain. Here He is arrested by the Grand Inquisitor, who fears that He will undo the Church's work of caring for all people as though they were children. The Grand Inquisitor berates Christ for having saddled man with the intolerable burden of freedom which Christ knew he could not bear. He tells Christ that the Church has rescued men from this insupportable burden—and men are happy, content, obedient. Only the Grand Inquisitor and a few associates suffer the torment of freedom. He tells Christ that He must again be put to death, for His teaching on freedom can cause nothing but misery among men. Ivan so tells the story that the reader knows the silent Christ is right, but his sympathy is also with the Grand Inquisitor who wants to preserve his contented flock from the curse of freedom.

History does not give a clear, unequivocal answer as to whether men want freedom. There is little doubt that we all desire personal liberties as long as they can be exercised irresponsibly. But thinking people know that the irresponsible freedoms of childhood must be put aside by adults, and that maturely borne freedom is a hard though satisfying thing. History seems to show that only a small portion of mankind prize freedom and are willing to accept its responsibilities. History also seems to show that among these people freedom cannot be completely extinguished. Four years after the appearance of *On Liberty*, we have observed, Polish leaders revolted in the name of freedom from the Russian tsar. Such revolts have occurred somewhere in the world, on a large or small scale, almost every year in the last century. They are witness that there have always been at least some men and women who are willing to risk their lives to regain liberties their forebears had surrendered or had had stolen from them.

Liberty has lost ground in the last century. This is not as distressing as the fact that no sounder "classic" has appeared to replace John Stuart Mill's defense of liberty. For the Grand Inquisitor offered a perfect refutation of Mill's argument twenty-one years after he published it. Mill based his case on utilitarian grounds, holding that liberty was a necessary means for promoting the greatest happiness of the greatest number. The Grand Inquisitor answered that freedom is a torment from which the masses pray for relief. If he is right, Mill's case collapses, for on utilitarian grounds just that measure of liberty which promotes the greatest happiness can be defended. Perhaps, contrary to Mill's argument, it might be the liberty of only one man.

This suggests that, in 1959, the case for liberty needs thinking through again. Personal freedom has its place in the scholastic tradition, as it does in existentialist thought, but it seems in need today of formulation in a classic work which will "catch on" as Mill's *On Liberty* did a century ago. It needs formulation in terms of Christian humanism if it is to be of lasting value, for freedom needs to be seen more as an obligation than as a right, though it is both—for each of us has the obligation to develop and perfect his human faculties, and we have the right to the means necessary to do this. It is not hard to demonstrate that one must be free to be a mature person—and all of us are created to achieve the status of maturity while still here on earth and to develop our distinctively human faculties as perfectly as possible.

Chapter IV

A Century of Liberalism

LATE IN 1859, Richard Cobden negotiated a commercial treaty with Napoleon III. The treaty, which reduced customs duties for both countries, allowed English manufactured goods to enter France at less than 30% duty, in contrast to the former prohibitive rates, and allowed French wines and brandies to enter England at greatly reduced tariffs. This trade treaty was hailed by Liberals as a great step toward achieving their ideal of a world market. "Our treaty with France," Gladstone observed, "was in fact a treaty with the world, and wide are the consequences which engagements of that kind carry in their train."

Earlier in the same year, Samuel Smiles published a conduct book based on Liberal principles. *Self Help: With Illustrations of Character, Conduct, and Perseverance* resulted from lectures Smiles had given to a group of young men who wanted to improve themselves and get ahead in the world. As the title suggests, it eulogized all those virtues connected with individualism and the Liberalism of a century ago: industriousness, thrift or frugality, calculation, careful investment, and the husbanding of time, capital, and labor. *Self Help* sold widely and was translated into several foreign languages. Its great success was due to its expressing in popular language the concepts that made up the prevailing Liberal thought of the age. Rather than proving his arguments by rational demonstration, Smiles used countless illustrations from the lives of famous men to illustrate his axioms and to "prove the case" for Liberalism.

Any well-known Liberal thinker of 1859, such as Cobden, Macaulay, or Spencer, would be dumbstruck to learn the principles that are referred to as "Liberal" in 1959. Liberals of the mid-nineteenth century held doctrines that today would be considered reactionary. They opposed public education and libraries as socialistic. They condemned unions as immoral and democracy as dangerous. Some of them went so far as to insist that not only sewer systems and all utilities but even armies and navies should be privately owned. They took very literally the slogan: "That government is best which governs

least." In 1959, Liberalism has a quite contrary
meaning. It holds for governmental guarantee of
security for all classes, for the regulation of business
in the interest of the consumer, for collective bargaining by unions. Whereas the Liberalism of 1859
opposed all kinds of welfare legislation, that of 1959
favors almost every form of welfare legislation.

In the following pages let us see how this great
reversal occurred. But first we must clarify what is
meant by the term "Liberalism," for it is used in
many different senses, and its meaning differs from
time to time and from country to country. Through
all the different meanings attached to Liberalism,
however, certain attitudes remain constant. Liberals
have always been opposed to existing authorities and
powers, and they have always favored whatever
change would limit these powers in the interest of
freedom for those suffering suppression. Thus Liberals in the early nineteenth century inveighed
against tariffs and other forms of governmental interference with industry, and in the early twentieth century they inveighed against "Big Business" in favor
of the consumer and of labor. Liberals, then, have
consistently opposed established authority, and their
positive doctrine has taken shape accordingly. They

have also consistently put great faith in man's ability to plan his future rationally and to create a good society.

The Liberalism of men like Samuel Smiles was achieved by a series of laws beginning with the English Reform Act of 1832, which gave control of the House of Commons to the middle class and enabled them to pass the legislation which made the "Victorian Compromise" of the mid-nineteenth century. The New Poor Law of 1834 gave them control of a supply of subservient labor, for this law forced the rural unemployed to flock to the cities to seek employment at subsistence wages rather than enter the work house on degrading conditions. In 1835, a Municipal Reform Act gave the middle class control of the government of English cities. Finally, a series of laws abolished the Navigations Acts, which regulated commerce on the seas, and the Corn Laws, which were sliding scale tariffs on grains. Thus, by mid-century, the Liberals had come close to securing their ideal of a world-wide free market, a free supply of labor and of raw materials. They had also developed a theory to justify their control of the government and the economy of England—as Liberals similarly did in France, where a Liberal regime existed from 1830 to 1848, and in other countries, where the Liberals were never able to realize their ideal as they largely did in England and, for a time, in the United States.

For the sake of clarity and convenience, let us refer to the Liberalism of 1859 as "Classic Liberalism" and to that of 1959 as "Welfare Liberalism." Between these two was a third variety, "Democratic Liberalism," which held for universal manhood suffrage toward the end of the nineteenth century, but did not go so far as to advocate the welfare state.

Classical Liberalism aimed at a world machine governed by universally valid "economic laws," such as the law of supply and demand. Its ideal of buying in the cheapest market and selling in the dearest could be realized only when the market was worldwide. This world-machine was to be powered by self-interest and governed by competition. Liberal theory held that self-interest would prompt industrialists and workers to labor in some mysterious way for the common good. Thus an industrialist who built up a prosperous concern would employ hundreds of workers and produce goods of excellent quality at a low price —all this immediately for the profit of the industrialist but ultimately for the good of all. Competition would guarantee that the best workers and the best industrialists survived, while the less fit failed. This, too, would promote the common good.

A market economy on a world-wide scale postulated an international division of labor possible only with completely free trade. Liberals believed that just as division of labor within a factory and within a country promoted efficiency and economy, so specialization among nations achieved further economic gains. Let England freely import raw materials from everywhere and specialize in manufacturing those goods in which she excelled, and let every other nation do likewise, Liberals argued, and then the lowest prices would be achieved. Free trade therefore became one of the cardinal points of mid-nineteenth century Liberalism.

Another cardinal point was that government should withdraw until it almost disappeared. Its sole job, Liberals believed, was to prevent interference with the automatic functioning of the market economy. This was to be accomplished by protecting persons and property from domestic or foreign aggression. "A wise and frugal government," Thomas Jefferson said, "which shall restrain men from injuring one another, shall leave them otherwise free to regulate their own pursuits of industry and improvement and shall not take from the mouth of labor the bread it has earned. This is the sum of good government. . . ." Liberals even went so far as to insist that the government had no right to require factory-owners to adopt safety devices, or pharmacists to put "poison" labels on bottles containing possibly fatal concoctions.

The arguments for a society governed by economic laws and protected by an otherwise do-nothing government rested upon a number of doctrines about man and society, which were extraordinarily intellectualized concepts bearing little resemblance to reality. The Liberals conceived of man as a calculating machine who carefully weighed reasons for and against every action before making a decision. They created that monstrosity, "the economic man," who was more like Univac than a human being with emotions, prejudices, and sensitivities, as well as reason. John Stuart Mill, for example, somehow believed that workers read reports of parliamentary debates every evening, kept track of the stock market, and followed international events sedulously.

In effect, Liberals denied the Christian doctrine of original sin. They believed that all men were basically good and rational, except that more education was needed to enable them to arrive at sound decisions. Each individual, they thought, was governed by self-interest, and was entirely capable of following this principle logically throughout life. They used Adam Smith's doctrine that self-interest and the common good are somehow identical to conclude that if each individual follows his enlightened self-interest the common good will somehow be achieved. Thus they were able to assert the sovereignty of the individual without concluding to the Hobbesian state of *bellum omnium contra omnes* or "war of all against all."

The Liberals of 1859 looked upon society as composed of these sovereign individuals. Each followed his own interest as the planets follow the law of gravity, and the good of all was harmoniously achieved. "The social problem is easily resolved," Frédéric Bastiat asserted. "Interests are harmonious—thus the solution is complete and entire in the word: *Liberty*." Society was held together in Liberal theory by thousands of contracts, which are the cement holding sovereign individuals together in social relationships. Thus buying and selling, employment and marriage, belonging to a church or a club, are all contracts that join individuals into societies.

Withdraw contract, [a Liberal of the age wrote]

suppose that no one can count upon anyone else fulfilling an engagement—and the members of a human community are atoms that cannot effectively combine; the complex cooperation and division of employments that are the essential characteristics of modern industry cannot be introduced among such beings. Suppose contracts freely made and effectively sanctioned, and the most elaborate social organization becomes possible, at least in a society of such human beings as the individualistic theory contemplates—gifted with mature reason, and governed by enlightened self-interest.

In 1859, Liberals believed in objective norms of right and wrong. On this basis they posited certain "natural rights," the most important of which were the right to property and freedom from external restraints. Liberals attached great importance to the right of property, for they believed it the mark which set successful men, such as themselves, off from the workingman and the ne'er-do-well. They considered property the basis of individual power and freedom, and they argued that the principal function of government was to protect property rights, an argument tersely put in the following words by Bruce Smith in *Liberty and Liberalism:*

If one man is allowed to call in a majority of his

neighbors to help him take, from another neighbor, part even of what that neighbor has legally accumulated, the latter will very soon cease to accumulate; and, inasmuch as accumulation necessitates the exercise of mind and body, which none of us really likes apart from what it leads to, men would, if such a course were systematically and persistently pursued, very soon cease to exert themselves beyond what was absolutely essential for their own immediate wants. By continuing the process, society would, undoubtedly, very soon find itself in a condition of primitive life.

Thus did one Liberal believe he had refuted Socialism! In even more extreme fashion Macaulay asserted that universal manhood suffrage would destroy civilization, for it would lead to a despoiling of propertied people by the unpropertied majority—and it is on private property that civilization is built. For this reason Liberals argued against giving the vote to anyone not possessing a substantial amount of property.

Liberals also believed in 1859 that the purpose of society was to secure for all individuals the largest possible amount of personal freedom. For them, freedom meant absence of external restraints, and they believed that the government's function was to reduce these restraints to the simple one of not allowing people to interfere with each other's personal and property rights.

In 1859, then, Liberals held a simple view of man and society. Both were looked upon as machines moved by certain easily ascertainable laws. Organize society to give these laws free play, they believed, and the best possible order will be achieved. Man is moved by the profit motive or self interest, which he calculates mechanically on the pleasure-pain principle, and by following this incentive he automatically promotes the good of all. Society is composed of autonomous human atoms who have cunningly come together the better to promote their individual self-interests. Thus society is much like a corporation, with the individual stockholders having a stake in the company solely for the profit they might make. Such a view of man and society implicitly denied those things which are distinctively human in the person, for it denied that he was a social being, that he is united to others by love as well as by contract, and that he is as much his brother's keeper as his competitor.

Within a century, we have indicated, Liberalism had turned inside out, as it were, and adopted completely different views. What caused this reversal? An answer to this question involves two sets of factors: those movements in the latter nineteenth century which countered Liberalism and tended to push it into the background; and those trends which were part of Liberalism itself but made it logically develop new and contrary doctrines.

Liberalism was not a doctrine to obtain the loyalty of masses of men in any country. Few will die for an equal sign or become emotionally attached to calculus. Many will die for homeland or for national prestige. After 1859, nationalism and imperialism made a greater appeal than Liberalism to the masses of people in every country, men who loved adventure and looked for a cause to which they might attach themselves. Nationalism and imperialism tended to smother individualistic Liberalism, for nationalistic governments could brook no criticism of their policies. Imperial Germany, Italy, France, and most other countries overcame classical Liberalism by emphasizing the group against the individual, and making the nation, race, or state the important entity, with the indvidual counting only as a cell in the big body. Imperialism won out over its Liberal critics, who believed in free trade and a world-wide market, because it appealed to the average man's love of prestige and

adventure. This average man was much more interested in whether Stanley would find Livingstone
than whether Standard Oil would pay a dividend,
much prouder to know that his nation's flag had been
raised at Fashoda than to find that Amalgamated
Copper had gained a point on the stock market. He
found Cecil Rhodes easier to idolize than John
Stuart Mill, the "Charge of the Light Brigade" more
moving than Bentham's "felicific calculus."

Liberalism was swamped by still other developments over which it had no control. One of these
was the move toward universal literacy and democracy made inevitable by the industrial revolution.
The trend toward universal literacy brought the
masses of mankind into the orbit of politics. They
could no longer be ignored, especially when universal military service put guns in their hands, for
governments cannot ignore men who read books and
have rifles. The coming of democracy meant the end
of classical Liberalism, which held for a restricted
suffrage and for control of the economy by factory-
owners. Moreover, universal literacy meant that
workers could read Karl Marx and other critics of
the old Liberalism. This put Liberals on the defen-
sive and forced them to make concessions of an
economic and political nature to their workers as

insurance to keep the capitalistic system in existence. These concessions necessitated a change in Liberal doctrine.

Another development which undermined classical Liberalism was the rise of the historical or evolutionary view of life in the latter nineteenth century. Classical Liberalism had postulated a set of laws which were supposed to be valid at all times and in all countries. These were static laws on the Newtonian model. But the historical or evolutionary approach suggested that everything is in a state of change, that what is true in one age is not in another. The historical method was applied to geology, biology, philosophy, theology, economics, and all other branches of thought. The obvious conclusion was that classical Liberalism might have been true in the early nineteenth century, but as conditions of life change so Liberalism must modify its doctrines. By the very nature of things, then, the doctrines of classical Liberalism could no longer be true by the end of the century.

The natural result of the industrial revolution also invalidated classical Liberal theory, which was postulated of thousands of small producers bargaining with millions of individual workers. Competition reduced producers to a relatively small number of large corporations and workers combined into unions, so that the mobility of labor and capital was no longer a fact. The gradual elimination of individual producers suggested that Marx was right in believing that the inevitable result of competition was monopoly, as competitors killed off their rivals and took over their markets.

Among the trends of the century which undermined classical Liberalism, a philosophical development known as "positivism" was perhaps the most important. Classical Liberals, we have suggested, believed in a normative order of right and wrong, of laws which were universally valid. Positivism was a philosophical system which denied the existence of anything more than the individual, "positive" fact. Thus truth and error, right and wrong were considered meaningless phrases which had no objective validity. Positivism ruled out all ideas of "natural rights" or "human freedoms." Positivism thus made Liberalism impossible, much as a baseball game is impossible unless players on both teams and the umpire accept certain rules of the game. There can be no game if each player makes up his own rules as he goes along.

Classical Liberals accepted the age's denial of

natural rights, which had been the firm foundation
for their original doctrine. Herbert Spencer, for example, stated that it "would be a waste of philosophy"
to explain once more "that there is no such thing as
'natural right.'" The French Liberal, Émile Faguet,
told his readers that "A right . . . can be nothing
but the result of a contract. Every right which does
not result from a contract is a pretension, or rather
mere nonsense."

The utilitarian basis of classical Liberalism de-
volved naturally into pure subjectivity, for on the
utilitarian pleasure-pain principle every moral judgment is a subjective judgment of personal like or
dislike. Objective norms are dissolved in this solvent
of personal judgment, a point well made by Michael
Polanyi when he explains how in place of objective
reason and truth are substituted passion and appetite
which

set men free from obligations toward truth and justice,
reducing reason to its own caricature: to a mere rationalization of conclusions, predetermined by desire, and
eventually to be secured, or already held, by force. . . .
When the judge in court can no longer appeal to law
and justice; . . . when in public life there is no moral
principle commanding respect; when the revelations of
religion and of art are denied any substance—then there

are no grounds left on which any individual may justly make a stand against the rulers of the day.

Utilitarian thought also undermined classical Liberalism by setting up as both norm and goal the greatest happiness of the greatest number. For when it can be shown that Socialism or perhaps a modified welfare state achieves that end better than does a *laissez-faire* government, the latter can no longer be defended. Once it was seen that the principles of classical Liberalism led to material happiness for a few and misery for the masses, the greatest happiness principle led logically to state intervention in economic life in the interest of the many.

Finally, classical Liberalism made some kind of a welfare state* almost inevitable, for it stripped the individual—in theory and practice—down to an autonomous atom with no natural social connections and no privileges by reason of his status in society. Before Liberalism was triumphant, the individual person belonged to many groups because of his position in society, such as the family, the guild, the parish, and the local community. Liberalism dissolved these groups or turned them into purely contractual

---

* We use the term "welfare state" in a neutral sense as a state which seeks to promote the material welfare of its people by such positive measures as social security legislation.

arrangements. Thus the individual could look only to the state for protection. The degree of liberty accorded to the strong and the wealthy by classical Liberalism naturally resulted in serious abuses, so that by 1880 or so most thinking men looked to the state to take a larger role in controlling "Big Business" and protecting the weaker, poorer segments of society.

The transition from classical to welfare Liberalism was a logical process, then, which occurred in various countries when industry reached a certain point of development. In every case there was a period of confusion as to what Liberalism meant and who were the Liberals. In the twenty-five years before World War I, welfare Liberalism in England took shape in the thought of men like Leonard T. Hobhouse and in the policies of statesmen like David Lloyd George and Winston Churchill. Older Liberals like Herbert Spencer shrilled that they were the true Liberals and that the new doctrines "masquerading" under the fine old word "Liberalism" were socialistic and destructive of liberty.

A similar pattern of transition occurred in the United States during the Great Depression. Advocates of the New Deal were generally considered Liberals, but such people as Herbert Hoover and his

Secretary of the Treasury, Ogden Mills, considered themselves the guardians of true Liberalism. In 1934, Hoover published his *Challenge to Liberty,* and two years later Mills published a book he called *Liberalism Fights On,* both attacks on the New Deal's form of Liberalism as subversive of true liberty. Thus supporters of the older classical Liberalism had become conservative, for they were defending a system established on this doctrine and they opposed any basic alteration in it.

Welfare Liberalism was formulated in the interest of what were considered the "little people" against "Big Business." It sought to protect workers, farmers, and consumers from the industrialist who had grown powerful and had considerable influence over the government. It advocated governmental reforms to give the masses of men a more direct voice in public affairs and to enable them to control legislation. Thus it proposed the direct election of senators in this country, the referendum and the initiative, and it organized labor and farmer lobbies to counter those of "Big Business."

Welfare Liberalism took shape in England in the first decade of the twentieth century and was adopted by American Liberals without substantial change about a generation later. In the first decade of this century, the new Liberals both formulated a theory of welfare Liberalism and enacted a series of laws which seem rather timid today but were then considered bold steps toward Socialism. They began by rejecting the classical Liberals' concept of man in favor of one who has feelings as well as intellect. But they weakened their case fatally by asserting that temporal society encompassed the whole of man's existence, thus making it impossible for a person to have rights against the state, since he has no end, no obligations, or rights which transcend temporal society. Moreover, on this positivistic philosophy, the new Liberals denied man any rights or freedoms except those accorded to him by society. The only grounds on which rights can be defended, with welfare Liberalism, is the utilitarian assertion that they promote the common good. For the final ethical norm for the new Liberals is "social utility," which itself is a changing thing resulting in a fluid ethics. "In taking social utility for a standard of reference for the values of effort and satisfaction," John Hobson explained, "we labor under no illusion as to definiteness or permanency." Somehow, he believed, each age will arrive at "a common grasp of what is for the good of society"—which puts individual rights and the human person at the disposal of an ever-changing public consensus of opinion. If enough people believe euthanasia or compulsory sterilization will promote the common good, the individual has no grounds in welfare Liberalism on which to stand against the new ethic requiring such practices.

Welfare Liberals thought they were safeguarding the individual, however, by holding that rule by law was the only valid form of government. Thus they condemned personal despotism and rule by popular tyranny, for, according to Leonard T. Hobhouse, "the first condition of free government is government not by the arbitrary determination of the ruler, but by fixed rules of law, to which the ruler is himself subject." As a matter of fact, although they undermined the individual's claim to personal rights, they were most sensitive in protecting the old freedoms. Welfare Liberals have stoutly championed freedom of conscience and religion, of press and speech, both in England and in the United States, to which they added such new "freedoms" as those of opportunity and of state-guaranteed security.

The classical Liberals' concept of property was fundamentally altered by welfare Liberals. Rejection of the older view of society as a collection of atomistic individuals, Hobson wrote in 1909, "completely explodes the notion of property as an inherent individual right, for it shows that no individual can make or appropriate anything of value without the direct continuous assistance of society." Welfare Liberals tried to strike a middle ground between complete Socialism and the older individualism by making a distinction between the social and individual contributions to property value. Increased property value not due to the individual should go to the state, for this was "unearned income"—such as inheritances, or increased land values because a community has grown up around one's formerly isolated farm. Welfare Liberals also advocated state ownership of industries which are natural monopolies, and close state regulation of the use of privately owned property.

One cannot help feeling that the reaction of welfare Liberalism from its classical predecessor went too far and was grounded on the shifting sands of a faulty social philosophy. It was right in seeing man as a social being and society as something more than a collection of individuals held together by a myriad of contracts, but it saw individual men as only parts of society who were nothing outside of it, whereas the older Christian tradition viewed society as a whole made of human persons who are themselves wholes and who have a destiny beyond temporal society.

It is obvious that welfare Liberals would increase the powers and the functions of the state considerably. In 1908, Winston Churchill said that he "should like to see the state undertaking new functions, stepping forward into new spheres of activity, particularly in services which are in the nature of monopolies." And Hobson insisted that the new Liberalism should "demand an interference by government with existing rights of private property and private business enterprise, and an assertion through taxation of public rights of property, so novel in character and so considerable in size as rightly to be considered revolutionary."

These ideas were worked into legislation that followed five main directions: 1) extension of state protection; 2) restriction of freedom of contract; 3) preference for collective as contrasted with individual action; 4) equalization of advantages among individuals; and 5) the use of taxation to redistribute wealth. Laws were passed in 1906 and 1913 to protect trade unions in peaceful picketing and in using their funds for political purposes. Minimum wages and maximum hours were set for coal miners and those in the "sweated industries." A Workman's

Compensation Act gave accident insurance to laborers, and an Old Age Pensions Act provided a small weekly pension for persons over seventy. Free lunches were given to needy schoolchildren, and the Children's Act of 1908 provided free medical care at childbirth and for young children. A Housing and Town Planning Act authorized public authorities to condemn unsafe or unsanitary tenements and replace them with parks or housing developments. A comprehensive National Health Insurance Act provided social security benefits for all workers making less than £160 a year.

New Deal legislation in this country followed a similar pattern. The Social Security Law of 1935, the Wagner Labor Law, and other such bills are too well known to require description here. It is sufficient to note that American welfare Liberalism favored unions against industry, advocated high progressive taxes as a means of redistributing wealth as well as raising revenue, called upon the state to regulate business closely to protect the consumer, and urged the government to undertake many economic functions supplementing and competing with private enterprise. At the same time, American welfare Liberals manifested tender regard for personal freedoms and called upon the Supreme Court to protect them zealously.

What has been the total effect of Liberalism in

the period since 1859? It has gone through a cycle from demanding a "hands off" policy by the state in the name of individual freedom to requesting an active role by the state in the interest of social security. In a sense, then, Liberalism has sold out liberty for security. Welfare Liberals answer this charge by maintaining that liberty is meaningless for the "little people" if it means liberty to starve, as it seemed to mean for so many in the mid-nineteenth century. By restricting the liberty of the "big fellow," they insist, they are actually giving the rest of us meaningful liberties. There is considerable weight to this assertion, and a good deal to be said against it.

Classical Liberalism played an important role in the history of the Western world before it grew conservative. One historian has written that the Liberal's "creed dominates the epoch, his faith gives it guidance, his works give it substance. It is his world, made in his own image." Many accomplishments of classical Liberalism were good: its dedication to liberty, its critical frame of mind, its constant searching for better social arrangements, its role in creating a formerly undreamed of quantity and variety of material goods, its tendency to break down class barriers, and its advocacy of such humanitarian legislation as prison reform and the protection of children and women. These were all good things. But these accomplishments were obtained at too high a price. For classical Liberalism was a social solvent that destroyed much that was good in the older society, along with much that was bad, and more that was a mixture of the two. As a social solvent, classical Liberalism tended to make man autonomous in theory and in practice. Put briefly, it replaced the person with the individual. For it denied man's social nature and overlooked his responsibilities. It undermined any rational principle for asserting personal rights when it described man as an aggressive, bargaining individual whose rights and duties rest solely on contracts.

In his Christmas Message of 1945, Pope Pius XII stated the ultimate result of Liberalism in these terms:

Here and there—at once the result of its [Liberalism's] destructive force and the hostile reaction to it—totalitarianism supplanted it. In a word, what was the net result after a little more than a century of those strivings? Human liberty buried; forced organizations; a world which for brutality and barbarity, for its achievement of destruction and ruin, but above all for its tragic disunity and insecurity has never known an equal.

By dissolving the societies that formerly protected

men, classical Liberalism left them individual grains of sand from which dictators in the twentieth century made their totalitarian cement.

Welfare Liberalism was both a continuation of and a reaction to classical Liberalism. It was instinctively a move in the right direction, for it held that society was something more than an association of individuals held together by contract, that the person is a social being and that he owes much to society and has obligations to it. But unfortunately welfare Liberalism had lost contact with the older Christian view of man and society, which has a solid rational basis for asserting personal freedoms and human rights deriving from a Source anterior and superior to society. Welfare Liberalism has no criterion for stopping short of Socialism or Communism if it can be shown that they promote material social utility better than does welfare Liberalism. Much of its program is good and necessary, but its philosophy leaves man in the rather precarious position of having to trust that the "common sense" of the citizenry will not carry it to the logical conclusion of a full-blown Socialism—and so far this "common sense" has tended to prevail in the Anglo-Saxon countries, which is one of the reasons to be hopeful about the century beginning in 1959.

Chapter V

A Century of Modern Nationalism

In the spring of 1859, Camillo di Cavour provoked an ultimatum from Austria, thus beginning the War of Italian Liberation. In three months the war was over, Austria was excluded from the rich Po Valley, and the first big step toward Italian unification had taken place. Cavour cleverly capitalized on Italian national feeling to have the natives of Parma, Modena, the Papal Marches, and other Italian principalities stage "spontaneous" demonstrations for incorporation into Piedmont under the "King of Italy." Two years later, the Two Sicilies and most of the Papal States were taken by Piedmont, and the Kingdom of Italy was created.

The driving force behind this unification of Italy was an Italian nationalism which had erupted in armed revolt several times earlier in the century. It was a modern form of nationalism generated in the French Revolution and spread throughout Europe by missionary French armies. It was, in effect, a secularized religion which demanded of its adherents blind allegiance to the national state and an unquestioning belief in the superiority of one's nation over all others. This modern nationalism had taken over many religious rites, replacing religious hymns with national anthems, for example, and religious processions with national parades. It called men to martyrdom in wars for national honor, and it claimed first place in everyone's loyalty.

Before 1859, nationalism had played a part in setting up a number of national states. The Greeks had used it to inspire their revolt from the Ottoman Sultan, and the Serbs had invoked it against the same ruler. Both groups had enlisted the support of European sympathizers and had achieved their independence in 1829. The Belgians had used national feeling in their successful revolt from Holland in 1830. Elsewhere, nationalism had been enlisted without immediate signal success. It had been particularly strong in the Italys during the romantic *Risorgimento* or "reawakening." Italian patriots recalled the glory of "Italy" in the days of the Roman Republic and Empire, in the Middle Ages, and in the Renaissance. Patriots like Mazzini and Gioberti called upon Italians to awaken from their lethargy, achieve independence and unity, and once again live the glorious life which was their destiny.

The romantic nationalism of the early nineteenth century was closely tied in with the Liberal idea that governments are subject to the sovereign people, and that all governments should be limited by written constitutions containing a bill of rights and liberties reserved to the people. This romantic and Liberal nationalism appealed mostly to university professors and students, to literary and artistic people, to the younger sons of aristocratic families, and generally to the middle class. They believed that government should be by intelligent persons like themselves rather than an hereditary class. They identified the welfare of the entire nation with themselves. *Tout pour le peuple, rien par le peuple* (everything for the people, nothing by the people) was their slogan.

Nationalism in the first half of the nineteenth century was idealistic and good natured. Italian nationalists, like Mazzini, accorded equal place to other national groups. Their object of attack was the absolute king and the irresponsible government, and, of course, subordination to foreign rulers. Thus the *bête noir* of Italian nationalists was the Hapsburg emperor who held Lombardy and Venetia, and indirectly controlled the other Italian principalities. Nationalism inspired local revolts in Italy in 1820 and 1830, and a general revolution in 1848. In all these movements the aim was independence and national unification, an aim not achieved because it was desired only by the intellectuals and the middle class who lived in the cities. After initial successes, the great revolution of 1848 failed in Italy, as it did in the Germanies and elsewhere, because it was spontaneous, ill-organized, and not solidly backed by the non-urban people.

In the first half of the century, then, nationalism was a strong force which accomplished relatively little because it was not harnassed and directed at specific objects. A dispersive, spontaneous force, it had exploded rather harmlessly. But, beginning in 1859, Cavour utilized nationalism in Machiavellian fashion to control it, much like electric energy in a battery, to direct it toward specific purposes and to make it enhance the power of the state. Bismarck utilized it to mold thirty-eight states into the German Empire under the Prussian king's aegis. The French government used it to build up a hunger on the part of all Frenchmen for revenge on Germany after the humiliating defeat in the Franco-Prussian War. The English used it to justify their ruling of "backward" peoples, as the Irish used it to justify their agitation for independence from English rule. Nationalism was one of the forces driving nations into the first World War and continuing hatreds when that war was done. Hitler used it to drive the German people into a state of national insanity, as Mussolini used it to justify his repressive domestic and aggressive foreign policy. This is the nationalism which was termed by Pope Pius XI a form of heresy, for it divinized a nation and in true theological fashion refused to admit any other God.

The nationalism with which we are here concerned must be distinguished from patriotism or loyalty to one's government and nation. Patriotism is a natural virtue. Nationalism is an intensified and perverted patriotism which is artificially cultivated by governments to secure unquestioning obedience from their citizens and a blind faith in their nation's superiority over all others. It involves a contempt or hatred for other peoples, and demands that all "loyal" citizens willingly and unquestioningly make the supreme sacrifice demanded by the nation. "Ours is not to reason why; ours is but to do and die" is a typically nationalistic slogan, as is the slogan, "My country right or wrong." The German *Deutschland über Alles* and the French *revanche* (on Germany) are other typical slogans of blind nationalism.

The artificers of this secularized religion had at hand certain factors they could use to set one nation off from others. One of these is language. A national language gives a people a literature, a community of thought and tradition which belongs to them alone. To a certain extent language even molds the way a people think. It both makes them conscious of what they hold in common as a nation and emphasizes their difference from other nations. Nationalists have consistently utilized language to give a nation pride in its tradition and its accomplishments, and to set it off as a distinct historical entity. Thus Herder inveighed against Germans using French in "polite society," and urged the teaching of German instead of Latin and French. The German language, he insisted, was a noble tongue fit for a brave and noble people, and it was the only tongue for expressing the thoughts and feelings unique to this people. At his instance, the Grimm brothers delved into German history and philology to find the spirit of the noble German people in their folklore. Similarly, during the French Revolution, Barère insisted that all

Frenchmen speak the same language with the same accent. Uniformity of language was necessary for uniformity of thought, he believed, and all Frenchmen must think alike.

The literature of each people became the vehicle through which a national tradition was created. And in each national tradition events glorifying the national group were emphasized, and national heroes were revered. Thus was Joan of Arc presented less as a saint than as a savior of France from a villainous English people. Thus were the exploits of Sobieski sung to the Polish people, and of Marlborough to the English. Through a national literature, Rumanian historians rewrote the history of their people and justified their longing for national independence, as Greeks and Serbs had previously rewritten their own histories to justify their claims for modern greatness. In their own literatures, each people emerged the greatest of all nations at one time in history, the savior and promoter of civilization, a people badly treated by perverse fate and deserving of first rank among modern nations.

A second factor utilized in promoting nationalism is religion. After Poland was exterminated as a state in the latter eighteenth century, for example, the Polish people developed an intense nationalism in which they stressed their Roman Catholicism as against the Orthodoxy of their Russian masters and the Lutheranism of the Prussians. Such romantic authors as Mickiewicz even likened Poland to Christ, a nation then buried but destined to rise again on the third day and, by its suffering, to redeem the other nations of the world. Because religious differences usually followed national lines, they could almost always be used to sharpen national differences. Thus Englishmen came to see Spaniards as "Spanish papists" and Spaniards to see Englishmen as "English heretics." English persecution of the Irish was more vicious and Irish resentment stronger because the one nation was Protestant and the other Catholic. In the early twentieth century the leader of the *Action française,* an extremely nationalistic society, insisted that all good Frenchmen must be Catholic—though he himself apparently was an atheist—because he identified "the eldest daughter of the Church" with Catholic worship.

But religion did not always serve nationalism. A religion that transcended national boundaries, like Judaism or Catholicism, presented difficulties to those who would make it a distinctively national affair. The nationalistic state cannot allow a religion to play its proper role as a critic of public morality and national policy. It must reduce the Church to a department of state and an agency giving moral and religious sanction to governmental policy. For this reason the nationalistic state has frequently made war on the Church in order to reduce it to a national church controlled by the state. Thus Bismarck fought his *Kulturkampf* against the Catholic Church in the 1870's, Italy passed a series of crippling anti-religious laws, and the French Third Republic issued the *lois laiques* which crippled the Church before the first World War. Thus Hitler fought undeclared wars on both the Lutheran and Catholic churches.

Religions, therefore, occupy an ambivalent position in regard to nationalism. They can be utilized to demonstrate national differences, but any religion true to itself must label nationalism a vice and a false religion. Ultimately, therefore, religion becomes a check on nationalism and a critic of its advocates, as Hitler found in the years before the second World War.

Another factor used in producing excessive nationalism is national humiliation and defeat. A nation must have its collective nose rubbed in the dirt, so to speak, before it can lose its good sense sufficiently to become completely nationalistic. Thus we find Prussia developing a full-blown nationalism after the humiliating defeats by Napoleon at Jena and Auerstadt in 1806, and again after the humiliation at Versailles after the first World War. In similar fashion, French nationalism reached its peak after the disastrous defeat in the Franco-Prussian War in 1870. As seems to be the case with individuals, so with nations a sense of inferiority drives them to irrational extremes which are expressed in aggressive nationalistic drives.

An intense nationalism was developed in France after 1871 by "super-patriots" who considered the Third Republic incapable of upholding French honor against Germany. Léon Gambetta preached nationalism to the League of Patriots and the League of Teachers, to rifle clubs and other such organizations formed to cultivate hatred against Germany. Paul Déroulède, who called himself "an old crier for war," followed in Gambetta's footsteps, and added a new note to French nationalism: that the Third Republic be replaced by an authoritarian government, for only under strong men like Louis XIV and Napoleon had France realized her true glory. Déroulède and his associates backed the unsuccessful attempt of the French Minister of War Boulanger to seize the government by a *coup*.

Boulanger's failure convinced French nationalists that they needed a doctrine to inspire their followers and hold them together. This doctrine was best formulated by the novelist Maurice Barrès, who as a young man had come to Paris from his native Lorraine "to teach Parisians how to hate [Germans]." Barrès wove together various ideas then current in France to formulate a full-blown nationalism. One of these ideas was the anti-Semitism of Édouard Drumont, who held that France was secretly controlled by the Jews. Their "valets" were the Freemasons and Protestants, through whom they bled the nation economically and betrayed it to foreign enemies. The Dreyfus Affair and the Panama Scandal, both involving Jews, seemed to substantiate Drumont's thesis for those who wanted to believe it.

Drumont's anti-Semitism, anti-Protestantism, and anti-Freemasonry were utilized by Barrès to justify the slogan "France for Frenchmen," and to insist that it is as impossible for a foreigner to become a good naturalized Frenchman as it is for a Frenchman to become a Chinaman. Barrès maintained that the nation is the individual writ large, and that if a man wishes to amount to anything he must identify himself with the national state, make its interests, its policies, its friends and enemies also his. Only thus can the insignificant individual achieve greatness. Barrès appropriated the idea of authoritarian government and the burning desire for revenge on Germany. He also developed a cult of the soil and the tomb, using the then popular idea of environmental determinism to attach Frenchmen emotionally to their homeland and to the heroes who fought and died in its defense. Finally, he stressed the sacred importance of the French language and of the Catholic Church as expressions of the true French spirit.

Charles Maurras succeeded Barrès as the leading proponent of excessive French nationalism. Maurras was a brilliant young journalist who became famous when he covered the Dreyfus trial and wrote vehemently against the young Jewish officer and in favor of the French army. "What does this man's guilt or innocence matter," he asked, "when the honor of the French army is at stake?" Maurras added the element of monarchy to French nationalism. He tried to show that the Bourbons alone had been "integral" nationalists, that they alone supported all the items or fractions of Barrèsian nationalism, for they were anti-Semitic, anti-Protestant, Catholic, authoritarian, and loyally French. For many years Maurras published a paper, *Action française,* and headed a society of the same name. This organization was identified in many people's minds with Catholicism, and by some even after it was publically condemned by Rome.* Through the early decades of the twentieth century the *Action française* shrilly preached hatred of Germany, insisted that French blood must be preserved in order to be spilled in the Rhine, and maintained that national loyalty must transcend all other obligations to become truly unlimited and absolute.

In the years before the first World War, the Third Republic systematically cultivated an intense nationalism among all Frenchmen. Carlton J. H. Hayes has well observed on this point:

Frenchmen are a nationality with a national psychology which has real roots in ancient, medieval, and modern tradition but which in latter times has artificially been pruned and trained in order to produce the perfect flower of supreme loyalty. . . . It is the French State, more than anything else, which has made them Frenchmen. It is centralized; it is respected; it performs many functions; it fosters national art as well as national economics; it interprets "liberty, equality, frater-

* *Action française* was condemned by St. Pius X shortly before the first World War, but the condemnation had not been published when the war broke out. Its publication was therefore postponed and the document of condemnation seems to have been mislaid. A new condemnation was prepared by Pius XI after the war and published in 1924.

nity"; it is democratic; it is republican, it operates in a "grand manner." The State may be conceived of as a metaphysical being, an idealized embodiment of a popular "soul," a mysterious supernatural agency of eternal human destiny; and as such it frequently finds lodgement in finite minds and thereby acquires a considerable quasi-religious significance.

Across the Rhine an equally intense form of nationalism was cultivated by German thinkers and fostered by the government to justify both Prussia's aggressive unification of the German states and the imperialistic policies of the resultant German Empire. Herder had laid the groundwork for later excessive German nationalism by insisting that the German people should not try to imitate the French, for they had their own language and culture, their own history and traditions, and in these they should take pride. Following Herder's suggestion, literary figures like Friedrich von Schlegel turned to old German literature, history, and religion to develop a haughty self-assurance among Germans and a pride in their culture. "Nothing is so important," Schlegel wrote, "as that the Germans return to the source of their own language and poetry, and liberate from the old documents of their ancestral past that power of old, that noble spirit which, unrecognized by us, is sleeping in them."

German mythology was revived. It was also revised to glorify all things German and to demean other nationalities. Meanwhile, the Prussian state encouraged the new history on the maxim enunciated by Minister of Education Humboldt: "The State must replace by intellectual force what it has lost in physical force." Thus the new history tended to glorify the nation, to see the past in terms of struggle between nations, and to make history a story of "good guys" and "bad guys," with one's own nation always the best of the "good guys."

But it was a philosopher rather than historians who worked out the basic formula for German nationalism. Georg Hegel was a philosophical idealist who taught that the state is the Divine Idea realizing itself in history. Thus at each moment of history the state is all it should be, since it is the Divine Idea, or God, objectified. Hegel taught that states are the ultimate reality in history, that war is natural and salutary as the best means of seeing which state is the best realization of the Divine Idea at any given time. "Napoleon," he is quoted as saying, "was the Divine Idea on horseback."

Hegel maintained that men can be free, moral, and manly only by obeying the state. Only in this way can one be his better self. Hegel and his followers held that men have a real will and an ephemeral will, and that freedom consists in following one's real will rather than the ever-changing ephemeral will. Each man is conscious of his ephemeral will, to which he can easily become a slave, but he finds his real will objectified not in himself but in the will of the state. Thus he realizes true freedom only in obedience to the state.

Hegelian thought was most successfully popularized by Heinrich von Treitschke, who fought for Prussia and Germany in the university classroom when he was excluded from military life because of deafness. Treitschke added little to Hegel's doctrine of the state, but he put it in graphic language which all literate persons could understand.* He justified imperialism, glorified war, and insisted that man has no more rights against the state than a cell has against the body. "The appeal to arms will be valid until the end of history," he wrote, "and therein lies

---

* Hegel was vague and obscure, a quality which seemed to enhance his reputation among German scholars. But few could read him. "There is only one man who understands me," he is supposed to have remarked, "and sometimes I am not sure about myself."

the sacredness of war." With very poor logic but very moving rhetoric he asserted that states are super-persons with superegos and super-wills. "States must be conceived," he believed, "as the great collective personalities of history, thoroughly capable of bearing responsibility and blame. We may even speak of their legal guilt, and still more accurately of their individuality. Having personality, the state must necessarily have the one outstanding attribute of personality, namely, will. And since the state must be regarded as *the* great collective personality, it must have the most emphatic will that can be imagined."

German nationalism was intensified and given a peculiar flavor by the journalist Houston Stewart Chamberlain and the philosopher Friedrich Nietzsche. Chamberlain was an unusual Englishman from a quite unusual English family. His elder brother, Basil Hall, had emigrated to Japan, where he married a Japanese wife and became the outstanding authority on Japanese philology. Houston Stewart settled in Germany. There he married the daughter of Richard Wagner, who besides being a great music composer was a German nationalist and racialist. Chamberlain popularized Wagner's ideas in a work entitled *Foundations of the Nineteenth Century,* an excursion into world history published in 1899 in which the author tried to show that all virtue and all creative genius are to be found in the Teutonic race. By distorting history, Chamberlain demonstrated that Teutonic blood was responsible for all great civilizations, for Christianity, and for such revivals as the Renaissance in Italy. He concluded that Teutons must be careful not to contaminate racial purity by intermarriage with Jews and Latins or by the adoption of non-Teutonic ideas.

Nietzsche is important for his theory of superman and his condemnation of the inferior man's morality as preached by Christianity and democracy. Nietzsche accepted the doctrine of evolution so popular in his age and proclaimed that the progress toward a better world rested in the hands of *Übermensch* or superman. He also insisted that all morality is relative. Thus war is good for the victor and bad for the vanquished. Democracy and Christianity, he claimed, uphold the morality of the weaker people, of the vanquished, and they must not be allowed to impede the progress of superman. Germans naturally identified themselves, following Nietzsche, with superman, and they tended to adopt the view that whatever aided their progress toward world domination was good from superman's and therefore from the historical point of view. The morality of Christianity and democracy was condemned for hampering superman and helping the inferior man to perpetuate himself in history.

All these doctrines were incorporated into Nazism after the first World War to produce the most intensely nationalistic and racialist doctrine known in history.

Meanwhile, nationalism played a significant role in precipitating the crises that moved into the first World War. Statesmen were condemned by nationalists for making concessions to other national states in the Moroccan and Balkan crises in the years before 1914. They were forced by nationalist-inspired public opinion at home to take an ever stiffer stand against each other and to develop the international relations which made war almost inevitable. Moreover, when war began, each nation sought to enlist the enthusiastic support of its citizenry by portraying its enemies in the worst light possible and by whitewashing itself. When the war was over and attempts to make lasting peace were undertaken, statesmen found it impossible to turn off the faucets of hatred they had opened full during the war. Thus it became impossible for David Lloyd George or Woodrow Wilson to tell their nationals that the

Germans were not really villains and that they had not intentionally precipitated the war. Thus it was impossible to obtain the kind of peace which would leave no festering nationalistic wounds in the twentieth century.

Between 1859 and 1920, nationalism developed more completely in France and Germany than elsewhere. Minor countries, such as Poland and Serbia, had equally intense forms of nationalism, but they were confined to small nations that could not independently change the course of history. In other places, such as England and the United States, there were occasional outbursts of national feeling, but in these countries the factors working against the heresy of nationalism were too strong to succumb. Palmerston's *Civis Romanus Sum* speech, for example, in which he tried to compare English citizenship in the nineteenth century with Roman citizenship in the time of St. Paul, evoked a flare of nationalistic feeling which soon embarrassed Englishmen and was extinguished. Similarly, American nationalistic feeling during the Spanish-American War was soon forgotten as Americans set about the more practical business of making more money and building up their burgeoning industry.

Other nations, like the Irish and the Scandinavians, failed to develop a full-blown nationalism because they had a solid sense of reality. As people with a poetic insight into truth, the Irish, for example, knew very well that the nation is not a super-being, that the individual and eternity are the great realities, and that there is something fundamentally wrong in sacrificing individual freedom for national license. Any people who will fight as volunteers but not as draftees, any people who believe the government is to serve them and not they the government, are not fit soil in which to plant the seed of national-ist doctrine. Thus while nationalism took root and grew prodigiously in some countries, it failed to achieve more than stunted growth in many places, such as the United States, England, and Ireland.

There is an axiom among students of nationalism that the most thoroughgoing nationalists are *aus-landers*, Irishmen in Boston or Chicago, Germans in Lithuania or Egypt, or Frenchmen in St. Louis. This is because nationals far removed from a country can extol its virtues without seeing its shortcomings and its weaknesses. The grass of Eire is greener to the Irishman in Boston than to the native of Drogheda, as the wonders of Germany are more wonderful to the German in Pennsylvania than they are to the taxpayer in Berlin. Thus the most enthusiastic nationalists at the time of the first World War and after were those who extolled countries not in existence, or foreigners who eulogized the nations in which they did not live. Polish nationalism, for example, was extreme with Poles who had not yet resurrected the Polish state dissected in the three partitions of the eighteenth century. The creation of a Poland, the enlargement of a Serbia into a Yugoslavia, or the breakup of the Austro-Hungarian Empire into many national states did a great deal to dampen nationalistic ardor among these people.

Among two European national groups, however, nationalism reached an extreme after the first World War. These were Germany, defeated and humiliated in the war, and Italy, cheated by the peace treaties of the spoils for which she was fighting. In each country a group came to power by utilizing this dissatisfaction with the peace arrangments and by taking advantage of the national inferiority complex in each country. In Germany, the Nazi leaders were almost all *auslanders*, Germans raised and living outside the country, who followed the Austrian Hitler to extol the virtue of the German people and to inveigh against their mistreatment in history. In Italy, an ex-Socialist became the ruler of the nation by appealing to the younger element in nationalistic terms and promising to regain Italy's national honor.

At first, Mussolini insisted that Fascism was a movement, not a doctrine, and that it followed instinct rather than ideas. But eventually he found it necessary to formulate the doctrine of Fascism, which became a new and a totalitarian expression of nationalism. Mussolini glorified the state, in Hegelian fashion, as the origin of all life. With him the state was totalitarian—a word which Mussolini seems to have invented—and all-embracing. The Fascist motto was: "All is in the state and for the state; nothing outside the state, nothing against the state." "Anti-individualistic," Mussolini wrote, "the Fascist conception of life stresses the importance of the state and accepts the individual only insofar as his interests coincide with those of the state." Thus the state is absolute; all else, including the human person, is relative and has being only insofar as it is incorporated into the state.

Mussolini rejected peace as a degenerate form of life and eulogized struggle. He similarly decried democracy, Christianity, and international movements to promote peace, for they interfered with the aggressive goals of Fascism. "The value of Fascism," he insisted, "lies in the fact that it has a will to exist and a will to power, a firm front in the reality of violence. The Fascist state is an embodied will to power."

Fascism was a form of nationalism immune from rational criticism, for it was non-rational. It was expressed by *Il Duce* who, Italians were told, was the ideal head of the nation because he possessed "infallible intuition." Fascists believed in the truth of "creative" rather than "reflective" reason. "Before all, I trust my insight," Mussolini told Italians. "What I call my insight—it is indefinable."

Fascism made a strong appeal to young Italians disillusioned with the first World War and with the middle-class materialism of the age. Against this Mussolini stressed an idealism and a call to virile, violent action which evoked popular response. But most Italians were too well balanced and possessed too good a sense of humor—which is another way of saying the same thing—to be taken in by Fascism. And when Mussolini passed ignominiously from history, only a small group of fanatics remained. They have had little effect on Italian life since 1945.

Under the volcanic leadership of Adolf Hitler and formulated by such theorists as Alfred Rosenberg, German nationalism took shape between the two world wars as Nazism. The Nazis wedded the idea of race to that of state to create the *volkstaat* or national state, which is described as "a permanent, supernatural, mystical entity, real beyond the existing totality of all its inhabitants." The Nazis maintained that the Aryan is the master race, and therefore rightly entitled to a political position of mastery over inferior, subordinate races.

In his campaign to overthrow the German Republic, Hitler employed every strain of nationalism developed in the nineteenth century. These he wove together to create Nazism. He used Wagner's and Chamberlain's racialist doctrine, seemingly made more "scientific" by the measurement of skulls. But the fact remained that anyone who agreed with Hitler was found to be Aryan, whereas those who disagreed with him were found to be contaminated with a measure of Jewish blood. Nazi theory held that "we think with our blood," that what is true for Jews is not true for Aryans, that values and norms differ from race to race. Hitler also appropriated Nietzsche's concept of superman and applied it to the Aryan. Further, he utilized the Hegelian idea of freedom to insist that an Aryan realized true freedom only in identifying his will with that of the state as expressed by *der Führer*.

How could Nazism, essentially irrational in its

glorification of will and violence at the expense of reason, be popular with a people generally thought to be reasonable and practical? Hitler capitalized on a collective humiliation and fear in Germany to work the people into a state of frenzied nationalism. He ranted against the senseless "guilt clause" which the Allies put into the Versailles Treaty attributing sole guilt to Germany for causing World War I. Hitler also played on the theme that the glorious German army and the good German people had not really lost the war; they had been "stabbed in the back" by Jewish traitors and other non-German elements at home. Hitler capitalized on fear by pointing to the threat of international Communism and promising that his nationalistic movement would save both Germany and the rest of Europe from this menace to the racialist national state.

By adroit psychology Hitler raised nationalism to a pitch of insane hatred. He and his associates developed and applied a psychology of color to evoke love, loyalty, hatred, and other emotions from their followers. They employed the tactic of the frequently repeated "big lie" and adopted the techniques of P. T. Barnum (whom Hitler studied closely) and American advertising men to sell their doctrines to the German people.

The resultant form of racialist nationalism known as Nazism replaced religion and objective truth in young German minds. It rewrote history as a story of struggle among the races. It preached hatred not only against Jews and other "inferior" races, but also against nations which impeded Germany's progress under Hitler to its "rightful" place of mastery in the world. It persecuted religions which criticized its venomous doctrines, and it put under the Reich Chamber of Culture all media controlling men's minds: radio, movies, the press, the theater, and the fine arts.

From the nature of the case, there can never be any accurate statistics on how many Germans were successfully indoctrinated with this excessive nationalism. Opposition was driven underground and criticism was stilled in men's throats. How much silent opposition and unspoken criticism there was we shall never know. We only know that many people joined the Nazi Party because they had no choice, and many others thought they could accept part of Hitler's program without endorsing his excessive racialistic doctrine. Although apparently millions of Germans—mostly younger people—were converted to this religion of hate, Hitler's tragic failure in World War II and his cowardly exit in his Berlin bunker disillusioned many of these converts. Since the Nazis did not monopolize German educational and cultural media long enough to control a generation's mind, when the war was over in 1945 there remained only a small number of Germans who were true Nazis. Most Germans could return to normal political and cultural life much as one awakens from a bad dream.

Since the end of the last war, nationalism has diminished in Europe. Educated people came to realize how large and vicious a role it had played in Western history, how it had promoted and intensified two World Wars, and how with it further wars were certain. Europeans came to understand that they were all victims of the same hatreds expressed in different languages. And they took steps to end these hatreds. German and French historians, for example, set up committees to correct their respective national textbooks on the basis of criticism offered by each other. Not only scholars but also statesmen and businessmen co-operated better on an international level after 1945, and it seems after more than a decade that Europeans entertain greater respect and good will for each other than they have at any time since 1859. In the last century, then, nationalism has reached absurd peaks of intensity and it has done great damage; but in recent years it seems to be diminishing.

Outside Europe, however, it is rampant. As the rest of the world adopted European ideas, techniques, and institutions in the last century, the so-called "backward" peoples adopted the idea of self-government as one of their rights. Under the rule of foreigners, with a culture, language, religion and tradition of their own, each of these peoples possessed all the materials for building a nationalism and for using it as the motive force in their drive for independence. Thus the drive of the Cypriots for independence from England in 1959 differs but little from the drive of the Greeks for independence from the Sultan over a century earlier. Only names, dates, and places differ.

Ironically, strong national feeling has made headway in that state which is supposed to transcend nationalities and to be the bastion of international Communism. For, under Stalin and his successors, Russian national feeling has tended to replace the more abstract, rationalistic Communist theory. Although Marxian Communism has never been officially repudiated, there has been more stress on the peculiar nature and virtues of the Russian people, the *Internationale* has been replaced by a typical national anthem, and there has been a good deal of propaganda that reminds one of the Panslavs of the Tsarist regime.

A decade after it took new shape as a hard-boiled rather than a romantic doctrine, then, nationalism survives in strongest form in the non-European parts of the world, where it is being utilized to justify and popularize movements against the domination of European masters. At a time when Europeans realize that nationalism has been a dangerous as well as a false ideology, it is being adopted by their cultural children throughout the world and turned against them, as it seems, indeed, that history has turned against them with the waning of imperialism in the mid-twentieth century.

Chapter VI

Imperialism: Five Continents
Into One World

ONLY THE perspective of another century will enable men to say with certainty what movement since 1859 is the most important and far-reaching. In 1959, imperialism seems to vie with communism for this distinction, and in several ways it can make a better claim than the latter for top place in importance. Imperialism was a movement whereby Western countries exploited the so-called "backward" areas of the earth, created "spheres of interest" in them, and extended them a measure of Western culture and religion with the result that they became somewhat "Europeanized."

There was an earlier age of imperialism, in the sixteenth and seventeenth centuries, when the European nations established trading posts in the near and far East and colonies in the Americas. Only in the Americas was European culture firmly established: the French version in Canada and down the Mississippi Valley, the Anglo-Saxon along the Atlantic seaboard of North America, and the Spanish brand through the rest of North America and all of South America. By 1859, most of the Americas had gone through the vicissitudes of empire and cut the bonds which bound them to the mother countries in Europe. A few areas had not achieved full independence. Canada, the only extensive land still a colony, was to achieve dominion status in less than a decade. These new countries combined with Europe to form an Atlantic community of nations belonging to the Western culture.

In the century since 1859, a wave of neo-imperialism has encompassed all of Africa, the second largest continent in the world, the greater part of Asia, and islands throughout the extensive Pacific Ocean. The pattern found in earlier imperialism has persisted through that of the nineteenth and twentieth centuries with only slight variations: exploitation of the backward areas, involving the emigration of some Europeans and of considerable investment; protection of these people and investments by creating "spheres of interest"; education of the native people in European ways with the result that they came to demand self-government; open revolt for independence as the last phase in the pattern of imperialism.

In 1859, the British enjoyed a considerable lead over other nations in the imperialist race. In the previous year the English government had dissolved the East India Company and took over direct control of its vast holdings. In 1859, English troops finally put down an Indian uprising and prepared the way for almost a century of control of India from desks in London. In the same year, England dispatched a considerable force to China to make that country accept a treaty giving England additional ports in China. The so-called "Chinese War of 1859" was a display of Western military force against a country that was backward militarily and industrially.

Despite these displays of Western power in 1859, imperialism failed to make notable headway for about twenty years, when it burst forth with a flourish to become the most important national occupation of several European countries. Until about 1875, Liberals held control of most European governments, and their policy was to concentrate on domestic reform and international co-operation. They believed that free trade was more profitable than imperialism. Moreover, until about 1875, war in Europe occupied the attention of all governments on that continent. With the conclusion of the Franco-

Prussian War in 1871 and the Russo-Turkish War in 1877, Europe enjoyed a period of relative peace which allowed the governments to release their aggressive energies for action outside the continent.

Other developments help account for the outburst of imperialism about 1880. The most important of these is the stage reached by the industrial revolution at that time. By 1880, such communication media as the telegraph and ocean cables had been achieved, and made it possible for a home government in Europe to be in instantaneous communication with colonial officials all over the world. Other technological developments, such as refrigeration, facilitated the use of colonial products in Europe, for now such perishable products as beef could be shipped from Australia to London, and canned goods could be sent from European countries all over the world. Moreover, technological progress had reached a point in the Western world to give a distinct advantage over "backward" peoples. Big guns and rifles were very convincing proof of the white man's superiority in the age of imperialism. And they made it possible for a handful of Europeans to govern millions of natives.

The industrial revolution had reached such a point by 1880 that it seemed necessary to look abroad for new markets and new sources of raw materials. Efficiency of production had made goods available on the home market to such an extent that in many lines it seemed that the home market was "saturated" unless increased efficiency could lower prices to include additional potential buyers at home. An easier way to enlarge the market was to sell goods abroad. Moreover, the so-called "backward countries" possessed a wealth of raw materials, such as rubber, hemp, and various minerals, which could be obtained at ridiculously low prices simply by extracting them from their source and transporting them to Europe.

The most important countries in the race for imperial expansion were Great Britain, France, Germany, and Russia. Lesser but nonetheless important roles were played by Italy, Belgium, Holland, and Portugal, while Spain tried futilely to hold on to its once glorious empire. The United States played a late but important role, picking up Spanish possessions in the Caribbean and the Pacific. In 1859, Great Britain had the most extensive empire in the world: Canada and small holdings in the Caribbean and Central America; Australia and New Zealand, as well as many smaller islands in the Pacific; ports of entry in China; India and Burma; South Africa; and such strategically located posts as Malta and Gibraltar for protecting the sea lanes to these imperial holdings. England was faced with the task of keeping these possessions—a task which sometimes involved taking new ones to prevent such aggressive states as Germany and Russia from threatening them.

France had completed the overpowering of Algeria by 1859 and was inching into the Sahara Desert to protect her holdings. She also had extensive possessions in Indo-China, the area between India and China, as well as interests in the near East. Russia had pushed eastward to the Pacific Ocean by 1859, controlling the Bering Straits, owning Alaska, and having made inroads toward San Francisco. She had also made overtures toward the control of the Balkans and an outlet to the Mediterranean Sea, through the Caucasus mountains to Afganistan and India, and northward into Siberia and Manchuria.

In 1859, Germany and Italy were not yet created. But as soon as they achieved statehood they were anxious to join the imperial race. As newcomers they were in the uncomfortable position of having to take the imperial leftovers or to cause trouble by ousting already established European controllers of backward lands. Holland, Portugal, and Spain held empires from earlier centuries, and their aim after 1859 was to protect their possessions from the more aggressive imperial nations. Holland and Portugal succeeded quite well, but Spain lost the remains of her empire to the United States toward the end of the nineteenth century. Belgium entered the imperial picture by acquiring a region in the heart of Africa many times the size of the mother country and blocking any scheme the British may have had of controlling Africa from the southern Cape to the Mediterranean.

Imperial action by the European powers after 1859 took place in three main theaters of action. One of these was Africa, unknown before mid-nineteenth century except for the northern Mediterranean coast, the southern tip of England's Cape Colony, and the western coast from which slave raids had long been made. Another was the near East: Persia, Afganistan, Asia Minor and the Palestine region, more important strategically than for resources, although oil in this region soon became a major factor in imperialist expansion. A third theater of action was Asia, including India, China, and the Pacific Islands, which were all important both as a source of raw materials and as markets for manufactured goods.

There has been considerable dispute as to which classes in the home countries pushed imperialist policies on their governments. The Marxist charge is that businessmen, stockholders, industrialists and the like were the chief instigators of imperialism. Businessmen were undoubtedly enthusiastic advocates of imperialist policies, and they organized associations such as the German *Kolonialverein* to lobby for their adoption. But businessmen were not extreme imperialists. They did not push their governments to the brink of war, and, following the dictates of "good business," they were willing to negotiate compromise settlements with rival powers.

Missionaries pushed the new imperialism, as they had pushed that of the sixteenth century. They wanted to win souls for God, and they saw imperialism as providentially opening up vast new fields to harvest. Livingstone ventured into the heart of Africa with no aim except to bring the blessings of Christianity to the native. There were thousands of missionaries with Livingstone's zeal but not with his self-reliance. These men followed their national flags into the backward areas and enjoyed protection of their governments back home. Hence they were frequently identified by the native with economic exploitation and armed occupation. That is why, when the Boxer Rebellion occurred in China in 1900, hundreds of missionaries were murdered along with

European merchants and soldiers—not because they were Christian but because they were European.

Churches in the mother countries gave strong support to imperialist advances, for there was a tendency in this highly nationalistic age for the Christians of each country to believe that their religion was better than that of any rival power. Even within one church there insensibly developed a nationalistic rivalry to cut out as large an area as possible to be a monopoly worked exclusively by missionaries of one's own nation. Many missionaries thus tended to identify their religion with Western culture and with the imperialist policies of their nation. In still another way did some missionaries promote imperialist expansion. Occasionally one was killed by natives when he pushed into the backward regions ahead of the flag and the army. His government often used his murder as an excuse to annex a few hundred more square miles of territory to assure "protection" to future missionaries venturing into the area.

Humanitarians also gave imperialism strong support in the mother countries. Many of them admitted an unsavory side to the movement, but they believed that it was "the white man's burden"—to use Kipling's phrase—to bring the blessings of Western progress to backward peoples throughout the globe.

Sanitation, medicine, good manners, and all the other blessings of Western civilization were to be buttered over the world, as it were, making it more habitable and happier.

Humanitarians and Christians supported imperialism for idealistic reasons, but they were not adverse to making a good profit while helping their backward fellowmen. How true this is Samuel Butler showed by publishing a satirical utopia, *Erewhon,* in which the supposed author tells of a wonderful land he discovered and suggests that a company be formed to enslave the natives and exploit their vast wealth as a preliminary step to Christianizing them. Thousands of readers were taken in before it was realized that Butler was pulling their legs.

Another group pushing imperialism were adventurers, men like the journalist Stanley, the office clerk Cecil Rhodes, and the traveller Karl Peters. These men entered the imperialist race with vigor and gusto, running for both sport and profit. Stanley, for example, concluded over 400 treaties and set up 22 trading posts in his race against the Frenchman de Brazza to control the Congo region. Rhodes, as another example, became the richest man in the world as he almost made his Cape to Cairo line of British colonies turn from a dream to a reality. Adventurers made imperialism a popular sport to the masses at home, who enthusiastically followed the exploits of their imperial heroes and marked their conquests by sticking little flags on the map.

Everywhere the most rabid supporters of imperialism were the masses of the people. They accepted uncritically the arguments of theorists like the German Heinrich von Treitschke that a great nation needed colonies, or the propaganda of newspapermen like the American Hearst who boasted that it was he who forced President McKinley into the Spanish-American War. The masses of the people enjoyed the vicarious thrill of adventuring into strange lands and the nationalistic pride of painting still another area of the globe in the mother country's color.

Politician that he was, President McKinley pulled out all the stops on the organ of imperialism and appealed to all motives when he played the following tune for reporters:

I walked the floor of the White House night after night until midnight; and I am not ashamed to tell you, gentlemen, that I went down on my knees and prayed Almighty God for light and guidance more than one night. And one night late it came to me this way—I don't know how it was, but it came:

1) That we could not give them [the Philippines] back to Spain—that would be cowardly and dishonorable;

2) That we could not turn them over to France or Germany—our commercial rivals in the Orient—that would be bad business and discreditable;

3) That we could not leave them to themselves—they were unfit for self-government—and they would soon have anarchy and misrule worse than Spain's war;

4) That there was nothing left for us to do but take them all, and to educate the Filipinos, and uplift and civilize and Christianize them as our fellowmen for whom Christ also died.

Although imperialism was supported by the masses of people, there was also a small group of rational critics of the movement in every country. Some critics were Liberals; others were Marxists. The former based their criticism on the doctrines of Adam Smith, who had argued that colonies are a nuisance and a burden, that they should be cut loose to bear their own cost of maintenance and defense, and that they are more useful economically as free customers and free suppliers of raw materials. Liberals believed that imperialism violated sound economic principles by making a world market impossible, for it fenced off "spheres of influence" as trade monopolies for one nation or another.

Liberal opposition to imperialism was basically a matter of economic theory, for the Liberal ideal was a world market with perfectly free trade among all nations—a logical goal for anyone subscribing to the economic theory of Adam Smith and his successors. But Liberals went on to offer other objections to imperialism and to prophesy such dire results as a world war if it continued to be the driving force in international relations. They pointed out its inhuman practices, its exploitation of the native population in backward countries, its expense to the nation for the profit of the few who were protected by the national army and navy while they amassed fortunes exploiting backward areas of the world. Liberals also showed that imperial rivalry was leading to a series of incidents and crises that were bound, some time or other, to result in a general war—as Norman Angell prophesied in *The Great Illusion* published three years before the outbreak of World War I.

Marxist criticism was even more trenchant. Communists maintained that capitalism could exist only in an expanding economy, and that the markets were saturated in Europe by the end of the nineteenth century. Therefore, they argued, backward countries must be exploited as new markets, as places for the investment of surplus capital, and as sources of raw materials for the expanding economy. Lenin and other Marxists maintained that imperialism was the last stage of the capitalist economy, and that native populations throughout the world would in time make common cause with the proletariat in the mother countries to overthrow the capitalistic yoke. The Marxist critique was not essentially sound—as we shall see later in this essay—but it contained enough truth to appeal to many intellectuals in the European world. Until the advent of World War I, however, critics of imperialism in every country were a small minority who were considered unpatriotic radicals.

Imperialist development followed a pattern which, with variations, prevailed in Africa, India, Asia, and the Pacific Islands. Motives pushing a country into the imperial race were the same everywhere: the economic aim of obtaining sources of raw material and additional markets so as to achieve self-sufficiency; the strategic motive of obtaining coaling stations and good harbors to maintain defendable lines of communications and to protect imperial holdings from rival nations; and later the simple motive of nationalistic prestige to show the masses at home how much area the mother country controlled.

The first step in imperial expansion was the simple one of extracting raw materials from the backward countries, such materials as gold, diamonds, rubber, and oil. This involved the European countries' obtaining "port cities" through which they tapped a backward country's resources. This, in turn, involved setting up an area in the port city in which European rather than native law prevailed and which was policed by the European nation. Almost always these "extraterritorial" concessions were a cause of friction between the European and the native governments.

Although the second step in imperial expansion was not originally envisioned, it came about naturally. Each imperialist nation found, in time, that it had to invest considerable capital in its business of exploiting the backward country: building railroads or highways to tap resources farther inland, constructing better harbors in the port city, or building additional dock facilities and living quarters to protect the original investment. As imperial rivals came to have capital invested in a given area, they excluded other nations by creating "spheres of interest" or monopolies for their own nationals' trading in the area under their control. "Spheres of interest" melted into "protectorates" as European nations split the rest of the world up among themselves for continued exploitation. Thus did England, France, and Germany mark off sections of China as belonging to one or the other for exclusive exploitation. Thus did England and Russia divide Persia into spheres of influence, or England and France draw lines of demarcation over respective areas in northern Africa. In each so-called sphere of influence the European nation maintained the sort of order which enabled its nationals to conduct trade on the best possible terms and which served to protect their investment abroad.

The third step in the pattern of imperialism was likewise not planned but was inevitable. This involved the development of a native "middle class" of clerks and other hirelings who learned the European language so they could read such signs as "handle carefully" or "this side up." A measure of literacy put these natives in touch with such European ideals as self-government, the rights of man, democracy, national independence, and representative government. For a native who can read "this side up" can eventually read John Stuart Mill or Karl Marx. When enough natives were possessed of these ideas, they took the fourth and final step of imperialism—a demand for independence which became widespread in the years leading up to 1959. Thus, a century after the English put down the Sepoy Mutiny in 1859 and forced the Chinese to open additional ports after the so-called "Arrow War," imperialism has been liquidated or is in process of liquidation throughout the world.

This liquidation has taken one of two directions. In some cases mother countries have granted former colonial holdings incorporation into the mother country, as France did with Algeria, or the United States did in 1959 with Hawaii. In other cases it has been won by violent revolution, as natives of French Indo-China did after World War II and those of north and central Africa have more recently done.

Imperialist expansion proceeded at an unprecedented rate in the last century and was a major factor contributing to the enmity of European nations in the period from 1859 to 1959. Italy, for example, joined the Triple Alliance with Germany and Austria-Hungary in 1882 because of conflict with France over Tunisia. When these differences were settled two decades later, Italy entered into an agreement with France which paved the way for her entrance into World War I on the side of Allies instead of the Central Powers. Again, when England and Russia settled their differences about Persia in 1907, it was possible for them to join with France in the Triple Entente before World War I.

Imperial rivalry caused the European nations to partition Africa, Asia, and the Near East in about half a century. Results for the natives were mixed. Their economic resources were exploited, sometimes bled dry, as in the case of rubber tree groves or mineral deposits. But this was no great loss to the natives who did not utilize these resources. In turn they were accorded the white man's "protection," which ran the spectrum from benevolent paternalism to barbarous enslavement. Some governments, especially the British, devoted much effort and many lives to protecting natives from white exploiters; others, such as the Belgians and Germans in equitorial Africa, devised inhuman methods to keep the natives at work.

Generally speaking, the natives were about as well off under imperial rule as they had been under their own potentates. But the imposition of foreign rule, with its alien norms and puzzling standards, was a cultural shock from which peoples throughout Asia and Africa have not yet recovered in 1959. It can be argued that Western standards are objectively better, but it can hardly be maintained that they worked out as an unmixed blessing for millions of people who were forced to abandon cultures their forebears had nurtured for centuries in favor of one they neither desired nor understood.

How fared the white man who carried the "burden" of imperialism in the last century? Individual fortunes were made, of course, like that of Cecil Rhodes in South Africa or the Doles in Hawaii. At what cost? Countless lives were lost in imperial adventure and in putting down native risings from year to year. Moreover, imperialist rivalry was one of the principal causes of the first World War. It is idle to maintain that there would have been no such war had there been no imperialism, but the fact is that imperialist rivalry sharpened international animosities and occasioned crises which brought war ever closer. And it was the clash of Austrian and Russian imperialisms in the Balkans that lay behind the assassination of Archduke Francis Ferdinand, the fuse which touched off World War I.

Did the European countries gain enough from imperialism to justify these costs? Grover Clark has answered this question statistically in his *Balance Sheet of Imperialism*. Advocates of imperialism insisted that backward lands were needed as new sources of raw materials. In 1937, colonial areas produced only 3% of the world's raw materials, rubber and tin being the only resources found chiefly in these lands. It was also maintained that colonies were needed to absorb surplus manufactured goods, but only a small fraction of any country's manufactures was purchased by their colonies, as most exports went to independent nations like the United States.

Advocates of imperialism talked much about *Lebensraum* or living space, insisting that colonies were needed to absorb the mother country's surplus population. But Europeans did not emigrate to the colonies to establish permanent homes, for imperial holdings were almost all in tropical regions not comfortably habitable for Europeans. The census figures of 1936 showed more foreign-born residents in New Hampshire alone than the number of Europeans who had emigrated to colonial areas in the preceding fifty years. Millions of Italians, Portuguese, and other nationalities emigrated in the century of imperialism, to be sure, but they went to the United States or Argentina or another suitable independent country.

Colonial areas did serve as an outlet for considerable surplus capital. In the four years before the first World War, for example, the British invested 17% of their capital at home and 36% in the colonies. The rest was invested abroad, as in rail-

roads and mines in Canada and the United States.
It seems, therefore, that imperialism failed to provide
the material gains which were promised by its supporters. Its principal payment was the national
prestige which it afforded the runners in the imperial
race, a prestige which gave fleeting satisfaction to
the home population in an age of aggressive nationalism, but which was purchased at the cost of ill-
feeling among the competitors and sullen resentment
from the oppressed peoples of Asia and Africa.

Wise men say that history does not repeat itself.
But they admit parallel developments which, though
not identical, are similar enough to justify comparison. Athenian imperialism and the spread of Greek
culture throughout the Mediterranean area were
similar to the neo-imperialism we have been discussing in these pages. As Greek culture was carried
from Athens throughout the Mediterranean world it
mixed with foreign elements to become an adulterated Hellenistic culture, a widespread civilization
encompassing most of the then known world, a culture basically Greek but no longer the pure classicism
of Athens. This extension of Greek culture was then
neither an unmixed blessing nor an unadulterated
evil.

Similarly, modern imperialism has resulted in the

spread of European culture throughout the world. In this comparison Europe replaces Athens, and the world replaces the Mediterranean area. As European culture spread throughout the world this last century, it was accepted in adulterated form by the natives of Asia and Africa. This is to be expected. For it is easier to understand Western mechanical accomplishments than the Christian's respect for human life. It is easier to adapt to the factory than accept Western man's veneration for womanhood. It is easier for natives to understand Marx than Christ.

The soul of Western culture is Christianity—a fact which many Europeans did not understand or denied through this last century when they were imposing their culture on the rest of the world. Thus it was an adulterated, soulless form of Western culture which spread from Europe to Africa and Asia after 1859. Christian missionaries tried to bring Christ with Christian culture, but they have been few in numbers and, despite their heroic work, they have made little more than a dent in the backward countries. Nor does baptism of itself bring complete understanding of Christianity and its culture. As it took German barbarians many generations to become thoroughly Christianized, so it will take natives in Africa and most parts of Asia considerable time to remold their cultures around the soul of Christianity, the facts of original sin, God-Made-Man, the Redemption, Mariology, the communion of saints, and Christ still living in His Mystical Body the Church. From these facts of the Christian religion customs and institutions develop, based on the dignity of the human person made in the image of God, and the rights he possesses as a creature transcending temporal society.

Time is required to develop such a culture, as it was required in the early Middle Ages. In 1959, then, we must say that the final results of a century of imperialism are not accomplished. At this date the peoples of Asia and Africa have risen against Europe. Some have turned with hatred on their former oppressors, as Red China, while others like India are more or less neutral as regards the European and American worlds. Still others, like Central Africa, might yet be won for Christianity. Bad feeling has been inadvertently developed among peoples achieving independence by the reluctance with which imperial powers release their grip on the backward nations. This plays into the hands of hot-headed nationalists among the native peoples, leaders who take advantage of the resentment against European masters to preach violence and hatred against them, a situation encouraged by the Western world's most formidable enemy, the Soviet Union.

In 1959, we live in the twilight of the age of imperialism. What its ultimate outcome will be no one can tell. But we are sure that imperialism wakened the peoples of Asia and Africa from their historical slumber and they wakened with a sullen hatred against their imperial oppressors. The future lies with them more than with the Western world, and they will carry into the future an adulterated Western culture, which they have turned against Europe in their struggle for independence and for a place in the world to which they believe their numbers have entitled them.

Chapter VII

A Century of Education

One of the great commitments in the Western world, and especially in America, this last century has been faith in the power of education to make the world a better and a happier habitat for the human race. With the vigorous exception of a few dissidents, most men during the past century have believed that if *their* type of education were adopted most social and personal problems would be solved. In almost all minds, then, great expectations were associated with the advance of universal, compulsory education.

Three events, symbolic of three approaches to the problem of education, occurred in 1859. In that year, Herbert Spencer published an essay which has been called by an historian of education "one of the most important works ever written in English." In it Spencer maintained that education in science was the most worthwhile type. In that same year, John Henry Newman published the second and basically revised edition of *The Idea of a University,* in which he presented the classic modern apologia for a liberal education. And in 1859 there was born in Vermont a certain John Dewey, who was destined to have greater influence on educational developments in America than either Spencer or Newman, for it was with Dewey that both the philosophy and the technique of "progressive education" originated. Whereas Spencer and Newman believed that education consisted of arriving at the truth, Dewey believed that it was primarily a matter of "life adjustment." Each of these three views of education was built around an aspect of the truth and had certain shortcomings—and they have struggled for power in the ever-expanding industry of education in the last century.

Spencer published the last and most important of four articles on education in the July, 1859, number of the *Westminster Review*. "What Knowledge Is of Most Worth" climaxed a mid-nineteenth century debate between proponents of the "old" or classical education and advocates of the "new" utilitarian training. It was published the next year with three other Spencerian essays on education under the title of *Education: Intellectual, Moral, and Physical*. This work was a "best seller" in its field for the next half century, being used in universities, normal schools,

and teachers' institutes, especially in the United
States, where Spencer seems to have been most influential. Some educators maintain that it was the
most influential book in the field. At any rate, it was
translated into thirteen languages and became one of
the most important statements in the great education
battle of the last century.

Spencer's argument is typical of the mid-nineteenth century. It is logical and, if you grant his
assumptions about the nature and goal of man, quite
convincing. Spencer was a self-educated man himself,
highly opinionated, a prodigious worker, and an independent thinker who had become famous for his
Social Statics of 1852, in which he applied to society
the ideas Darwin was to make famous in 1859 with
his *Origin of Species*. Spencer had picked up Mal-
thus' idea of population and Ricardo's economics of
scarcity to conclude that in the great struggle of life
nature ensures progress by eliminating the less fit.

It seems hard [he wrote in *Social Statics*] that a
laborer incapacitated by sickness from competing with
his stronger fellows, should have to bear the resulting
privations. It seems hard that widows and orphans
should be left to struggle for life or death. Nevertheless
when regarded not separately but in connection with
the interests of universal humanity, these harsh fatalities

are seen to be full of beneficence—the same beneficence which brings to early graves the children of diseased parents, and singles out the intemperate and the debilitated as the victims of an epidemic.

This law of nature makes progress inevitable. For, Spencer tells us, it "is due to the working of a universal law . . . and in virtue of that law it must continue until the state we call perfection is reached. . . . The advent of such a state is removed out of the region of probability into that of certainty. . . . Progress is not an accident, not a thing within human control, but a beneficent necessity."

Thus, the Spencer who wrote about education in 1859 was an insistent advocate of competition as a struggle for survival among men, and a convinced believer in inevitable progress. As an individualist he had already condemned public education as a form of socialism, and through his later life he fought as immoral each proposal for public support of libraries and schools. In typical "logical" fashion he stated his position in *Social Statics*: "Inasmuch as the taking away, by government, of more of a man's property than is needful for maintaining his rights, is an infringement of his rights, and therefore a reversal of the government's function towards him; and inasmuch as the taking away of his property to educate his own or other people's children is not needful for the maintaining of his rights; the taking away of his property for such a purpose is wrong."

"What Knowledge Is of Most Worth" becomes a simple logical demonstration for such a man as Spencer. He begins by telling us that since the purpose of education is "to prepare us for complete living," the proper way to evaluate a course of education is to list the needs and activities of life in their order of importance and then to see how completely this course prepares us to satisfy such needs and perform such activities. Spencer composes the following list, in order of importance, about which he tells the reader there is no longer any dispute: "1. Those activities which directly minister to self-preservation; 2. Those activities which, by securing the necessaries of life, indirectly minister to self-preservation; 3. Those activities which have for their end the rearing and discipline of offspring; 4. Those activities which are involved in the maintenance of proper social and political relations; 5. Those miscellaneous activities which make up the leisure part of life, devoted to the gratification of the tastes and feelings."

With such groundwork laid on the purpose of education and importance of various "life activities," it was easy for Spencer to demonstrate that courses in science are "always most useful for preparation for life" and therefore the type of knowledge of most worth. He further showed that besides having the most valuable content, courses in science do the best job of training the memory, judgment, and will. By "science," it should be noted, Spencer included such social sciences as economics, using the term in contrast to literary and humanistic studies like poetry or Greek. Spencer concludes his essay by telling the reader: "Thus to the question with which we set out —What knowledge is of most worth?—the uniform reply is—Science. This is the verdict on all the counts. For direct self-preservation . . . for that indirect self-preservation which we call getting a livelihood . . . for that interpretation of national life, past and present, without which the citizen cannot rightly regulate his conduct . . . for the most perfect production and highest enjoyment of art in all its forms . . . and for purposes of discipline— intellectual, moral, religious—the most efficient study is—Science."

Spencer is typically mid-nineteenth century in shedding the pedestrian boots of Science in favor of poetic wings in his last paragraph, as Darwin did in the *Origin*:

Paraphrasing an Eastern fable, we may say that in the family of knowledges, Science is the household drudge, who, in obscurity, hides unrecognized perfections. To her has been committed all the work; by her skill, intelligence, and devotion, have all the conveniences and gratifications been obtained; and while ceaselessly occupied ministering to the rest, she has been kept in the background, that her haughty sisters might flaunt their fripperies in the eyes of the world. The parallel holds yet further. For we are fast coming to the *dénouement*, when the positions will be changed; and while these haughty sisters sink into merited neglect, Science, proclaimed as highest alike in worth and beauty, will reign supreme.

Discussion on what is wrong with education in 1959 would almost imply that no one had listened to Spencer in the century since he proclaimed that courses in science were of the greatest worth. For technological competition with the Soviet Union has led many Americans to insist that we start teaching sciences too late, that we neglect them in favor of "useless" subjects, and that greater prominence must be given to science in the curriculum from primary grades through graduate school in the university. The technological revolution has undoubtedly made the need of highly specialized scientists acute and has given rise to the problem of how to produce such specialists without sacrificing those broader aspects of education which seem essential to a Christian, democratic way of life.

The second edition of a classic defense of "liberal education" appeared in 1859. Newman's *The Idea of a University* continues to be read and admired by those who believe in its arguments, but there is serious doubt that it has converted many "practical" men who believe that education is primarily intended to prepare a student to earn a living. Most people evade Newman's basic argument by replying that his type of liberal education is all right for those who have time and money to afford it, but that in our world it is a luxury which few can afford. There is something to this reply, since Newman lived and wrote in a world where men who went to college did have the leisure to obtain a liberal education. The question shifts to whether a society which demeans a liberal education is rightly organized. But first let us see what Newman's *Idea* was.

The book grew out of a failure. Newman had been asked by the Irish bishops to establish a Catholic university in Ireland. In 1852, he delivered a series of lectures in Dublin to people backing the proposed university, in which he tried to explain the nature of university education as distinct from vocational training on the one hand and spiritual training on the other. His basic point is that the primary end of education is to develop the mind rather than the soul or some special skill. Because the Irish bishops looked upon education as apologetics and spiritual development, they considered Newman a typical Englishman trying to force the Oxford system upon them. Newman's Irish adventure thus ended in dismal failure, but his lectures were published in 1852 as *The Idea of a University* and were thoroughly revised in 1859 to add, Newman tells us, to the force and clearness of his argument.

Newman defended "liberal" education against the utilitarian attacks of men like Spencer. Its purpose, he held, was not to pack the mind with millions of unrelated facts, but "to form the mind." "Our desideratum," he explained to his audience, "is the force, the steadiness, the comprehensiveness and the versatility of intellect, the command over our own powers, the instinctive just estimate of things as they pass before us. . . . A truly great intellect is one which takes a connected view of old and new, past and present, far and near, and which has an insight into the influence of all these one on another." Newman distinguishes a liberal education from dilettantism or brilliant, superficial views about everything, as well as from excessive specialization in a single area of knowledge at the cost of ignoring the rest.

A liberal education, in Newman's mind, is primarily the formation of the intellect so that it knows its way around in all fields of knowledge, so to speak, so that it can continue the adventure of learning safely throughout life. It is a mind that sees each item of knowledge in perspective, in relation to the total body of human knowledge. But liberal education is more than "know how" in the field of learning. It is also a more than superficial acquaintance with the major branches of learning, those sciences which deal with nature, man, and God. A liberal education must include all these areas for completeness and for balance. When ethics is eliminated from the curriculum, for example, "its territory would soon disappear, under a treaty of partition, as it may be called, between law, political economy, and physiology." The sciences balance and correct each other, and any education which does not include courses in theology, as well as the social and natural sciences, is lopsided.

This is the argument of the first half of *The Idea of a University*, summed up by Newman in this way:

I have argued in its [theology's] behalf, first, from the consideration that, whereas it is the very profession of a University to teach all sciences, on this account it cannot exclude Theology without being untrue to its profession. Next, I have said that, all sciences being connected together, and having bearings one on another, it is impossible to teach them all thoroughly, unless they all are taken into account, and Theology among them. Moreover, I have insisted on the important influence, which Theology in matter of fact does and must exercise over a great variety of sciences, completing and correcting them; so that, granting it to be a real science occupied upon truth, it cannot be omitted without great prejudice to the teaching of the rest. And lastly, I have urged that, supposing Theology be not taught, its province will not simply be neglected, but will be actually usurped by other sciences, which will teach, without warrant, conclusions of their own in a subject-matter which needs its own proper principles for its due formation and disposition.

The last part of the work shows that a liberal education is an end in itself, that entirely apart from any utility it might possess it is a good to be sought for its own sake. Newman's defense of liberal education is a spirited rebuttal of utilitarians who had been decrying all subjects which did not immediately prepare a student to earn a living. He insisted that developing the intellect was a good in itself, and that in a large sense it was most useful, inasmuch as it prepared one to follow his professional calling more successfully. No matter what occupation one might later follow, Newman argues, it is good to have developed that habit of mind "of which the attributes are freedom, equitableness, calmness, moderation, and wisdom." This is the aim of liberal education.

In an almost poetic passage Newman describes the product of a liberal education, the well formed mind of the gentleman:

The intellect, which has been disciplined to the perfection of its powers, which knows, and thinks while it knows, which has learned to leaven the dense mass of facts and events with the elastic force of reason, such an intellect cannot be partial, cannot be exclusive, cannot be impetuous, cannot be at a loss, cannot but be patient, collected, and majestically calm, because it discerns the end in every beginning, the origin in every end, the law in every interruption, the limit in each delay; because it ever knows where it stands, and how its path lies from one point to another. . . . It is almost prophetic from its knowledge of history; it is almost heart-searching from its knowledge of human nature; it has almost supernatural charity from its freedom from littleness and prejudice; it has almost the repose of faith, because nothing can startle it; it has almost the beauty and harmony of heavenly contemplation, so intimate is

it with the eternal order of things and the music of the
spheres.

The most frequently voiced criticism against Newman's advocacy of liberal education is that it is a beautiful but unattainable ideal. Newman wrote for gentlemen of leisure who never had to earn a living, the argument runs, and he wrote for an age when it was still possible for a well read man to keep abreast of developments in almost all branches of knowledge. But in 1959, the argument continues, everyone must earn his living and he must prepare to do this by specialization in college. The campuses are combed for graduating engineers, geologists, and accountants, but industrial recruiters do not ask for young men with the mind Newman describes as "liberal." They look for young men who know "how to do" something or other. Entirely apart from its impracticality, the argument against Newman goes on, knowledge has advanced and is advancing at such a furious pace that the ideal of having more than a superficial acquaintance with fields of thought outside one's specialty is simply unattainable.

There is no easy answer to these objections. Advocates of a liberal education maintain that by a properly balanced curriculum it is possible to cultivate the type of mind Newman labelled "liberal." They admit that ordinarily the young man or woman with a "liberal education" must go on to specialize in some area to obtain professional competence and skill. But, they insist—and this is the crux of the argument—such an investment in time and money is well made, both for the individual, for his field of later specialization, and for society at large. The side one takes in this argument is predetermined by one's sense of values and philosophy of education. If education is conceived of as training in a skill in order to earn a living, then Newman's argument makes no appeal. If it is looked upon in the Christian humanistic light, then his argument is forceful and compelling, and one wonders whether a society in which Newman's ideal is difficult to realize is well organized and motivated by right principles.

Another objection to Newman's ideal of liberal education is that it assumes an intellectual aristocracy which is repugnant in our democratic society. Such an objection, however, makes of democracy and education a levelling-down process, whereby all talents and ability are reduced to the least common denominator. Advocates of Newman's system of liberal education must concede, however, that it is not for the masses of mankind—nor was it ever so intended. In the specialization of labor which prevails in 1959, liberal education must be reserved for those who are intellectually able to take it and who see the value they receive for the time, effort, and money they invest in it.

Perhaps the most influential philosopher and educator in America in the last century was John Dewey. Born in 1859 in Burlington, Vermont, Dewey was one of the few thinkers in the last century who lived to see his ideas widely adopted and to lose their influence. For Dewey's theories and techniques of progressive education were in decline before he died in his ninety-third year in 1952.

Dewey was primarily a philosopher who looked upon the school as the laboratory where his philosophical ideas were to be tried and where society was to be remade according to his "instrumentalist" thought. Although Dewey never repudiated "progressive" educators who went to extremes in applying his basic principles, progressive education, nevertheless, frequently became a caricature of what Dewey had in mind. He must have been embarrassed, for example, to hear one admirer assert at his seventieth birthday celebration that "we think of Professor Dewey as the most profound and understanding thinker on education that the world has yet known," and, he went on, Plato's *Republic* was the most important book ever written on education "until John Dewey wrote his *Democracy and Education.*"

Despite such exaggerations, it must be admitted that Dewey is indirectly and partly responsible both for many improvements in educational practice and for many problems of "child-centered" education with a minimum of subject matter and absolutely no discipline. Through the strategically situated Teachers' College of Columbia University, Dewey came to influence superintendents and administrators of school systems throughout the country. William H. Kilpatrick, who as professor of education at Teachers' College did more than anyone to apply Dewey's theories to education, said in 1929 that "school life everywhere in our country and in many distant parts is finer and sweeter and more fruitful because of what he has taught." To this should be added that the "Blackboard Jungle" and the need to have policemen patrol high school corridors is also indirectly and partly attributable to John Dewey.

We have observed that Dewey was a philosopher by profession, but always maintained a lively interest in formal education because he considered the school the laboratory in which philosophers can conduct "controlled experiments" to verify their hypotheses and obtain new data. Education is also the medium through which philosophy operates to reconstruct society. This is what Dewey has in mind when he tells us that philosophy is a general theory of education, and that his *Democracy and Education* is the book in which his philosophy "was most fully expounded."

Dewey's most widely read book, however, was *The School and Society*, in which one finds the earliest exposition of what is loosely referred to as "progressive education." Dewey's original purpose was to supply in the school certain elements of training and education that children no longer received at home or in the neighborhood. Back in Dewey's boyhood in Vermont, boys and girls engaged in a number of household and farmyard chores, worked with their hands, made and did things. Dewey believed that he learned more at these chores than he did in school. By the time he was teaching at the University of Chicago he saw how industrialization had taken children out of household and neighborhood jobs, and thus, he believed, it took away from childhood training in habits of order and industry, acquaintance with the making of things by the transformation of raw materials into useful products. He further believed that in the modern industrial world these things could be supplied only by the school.

The existing system of education, Dewey insisted, was a waste of human life. Unconcerned with the child's "present," it pretended to prepare him for the "future." But it failed even to do this. "Our present education . . . is highly specialized, one sided and narrow," Dewey tells us. "It is an education dominated almost entirely by the medieval conception of learning. It is something which appeals for the most part simply to the intellectual aspect of our natures, our desire to learn, to accumulate information, and to get control of the symbols of learning; not to our impulses and tendencies to make, to do, to create, to produce, whether in the form of utility or of art." Education must undergo the same transformation society has undergone, and, Dewey believed, it must be an "open" affair like his philosophy, with no absolutes controlling it and no ends outside itself, instrumentalist in philosophy, scientific in methodology, societal in purpose.

The aim of education is given by Dewey in a number of ways. For one thing, it is to promote "child growth in a social institution." For another, it is to affiliate the school with life, to make it a "miniature society," an "embryonic community." Again, in Dewey's words: "The aim . . . is the development of social power and insight. It is this liberation from narrow utilities, this openness to the possibilities of the human spirit that makes these practical activities in the school allies of art and centers of science and history." Deweyites and educationists have created an "inner-sanctum" lingo of exciting terminology which perplexes and confuses us who use words in their traditional sense and are used to thinking in traditional ways. But it does not seem unjust to say that behind all these avowed purposes of education is the ulterior aim of using the school system as a tool for social engineering so as to produce the kind of society which the Deweyites think we should have.

Dewey defines education as "the process of experiencing." Again he writes: "Education may be defined as a process of the continuous reconstruction of experience, with the purpose of widening and deepening its social content, while at the same time the individual gains control of the methods involved." The school, at any rate, is to furnish the problems whose solution is "imperiously demanded" by the pupil's nature. The school is a social institution, "a part of the total social process." Education is a social affair, Dewey writes at great length, because the school must be a miniature of real life, which is social; because things have meaning only in their social setting; because the school is the means whereby society insures its continuance and works for its improvement; and because education is best achieved by a "sharing of experiences" by the pupils. Education is therefore a function of society, and schools are the means whereby society performs this function. The school must therefore—to use educationist terminology—be in vital interaction with the surrounding natural and social environment. Classes should be taken on field trips through factories in the neighborhood; the students should take active part in clean-up campaigns; and the administration should be sensitive to social pressures and opinions in the neighborhood.

Such relationship requires educators to be committed to certain social institutions and to a program for a "better society," for, as Dewey has remarked, "the conception of education as a social process and function has no definite meaning until we define the kind of society we have in mind." As we have already seen, Dewey favors democracy, something approaching a Welfare State which would still be an open society with a maximum of freedom for all. Dewey and his followers have been pronounced secularists, and many of them have attempted to impose their secularism on the public schools as the "American faith." At any rate, although instrumentalist philosophy holds that there can be no absolutes and that inquiry must proceed without an end in view, nevertheless the social function of the school has required educators to accept certain social ideas as at least temporarily absolute.

Thus education comes to be a form of social engineering. In his first work on education, Dewey insisted that "it is the business of every one interested in education to insist upon the school as the primary and most effective interest of social progress and reform. . . . The teacher is engaged, not simply in the training of individuals, but in the formation of proper social life. . . . In this way the teacher always is the prophet of the true God and the usherer in of the true kingdom of God."

Some educators have assumed this self-assigned burden of social engineering to "re-create" the student according to a social pattern of modern naturalism and secularism which is to be perfectly "neutral" on all religious and moral questions. Thus some of them have insisted that all children must be educated in the public school system, and that private schools are "dangerous" and "divisive." Others go so far as to demand that children be in school all day twelve months a year—which would obviously give educationists something close to a monopoly over all Americans' minds in their formative years.*

Dewey had many things to say about the school itself, its organization, curriculum, and physical facilities—and many of his observations were very shrewd criticisms of shortcomings in the older system. He opposed memory work and the forced accumulation of information about matters that were of no personal interest for the student. He insisted that since knowledge is an active affair, every school must be an "activity school" in which the students learn by doing. The basic reform in this respect is the replacement of the old "subject-centered" education, to which all students had to conform, with a "child-centered" education to which the curriculum and all other educational paraphernalia must conform. "Now the change which is coming into our education," he wrote in *The School and Society,* "is the shifting of the center of gravity. It is a change, a revolution, not unlike that introduced by Copernicus when the astronomical center shifted from the earth

---

* Some educators innocently and naïvely advocate this program following the "businessman" school of thought, which holds that classrooms should be utilized to the full. Others advocate it in order to control their students' lives completely.

to the sun. In this case the child becomes the sun about which the appliances of education revolve; he is the center about which they are organized."

There was undeniable need for reform in the older method of education. But unfortunately Dewey —and even more his followers—threw the baby out with the bath water. Dewey made it clear he had no intention of pandering to every student whim in concentrating on subjects which would interest him, nor did he intend to turn schools into mere mechanical workshops at the expense of intellectual activity. But he took the first step in this direction, and many of his educationist followers have rushed headlong in the direction he first indicated—with results we all know too well: courses in how to pick your dentist, how to do parlor stunts, what to do on a date, and other such social "musts" in place of Cicero, trigonometry, medieval history, and other older subjects supposedly barren of student interest.

Dewey did not personally advocate such specific courses, but he lived to see them employed and—as far as we know—he did not repudiate them. They seem logical applications of what he wrote about curriculum in *My Pedagogic Creed*. Here he gives us the principles for organizing the curriculum rather than drawing up a course of studies himself. "The only way to make the child conscious of his social heritage is to enable him to perform those fundamental types of activity which make civilization what it is." This includes such things as sewing, cooking, and manual training. But, Dewey goes on to warn us, "there is no succession of studies in the ideal school curriculum. If education is life, all life has, from the outset, a scientific aspect, an aspect of art and culture, and an aspect of communication. It cannot, therefore, be true that the proper studies of one grade are mere reading and writing, and that at a later grade, reading, or literature, or science, may be introduced. The progress is not in the succession of studies, but in the development of new attitudes towards, and new interests in, experience."

A century after Dewey's birth there is still no agreement on what kind of education is of most worth in the contemporary world. Through the greater part of the last century, most people put unquestioning faith in education as the means of resolving the world's social, political, and moral problems. But by 1959 this faith has dimmed somewhat, and many people are skeptical of what education can accomplish in a democratic society, partly, it would seem, because too much has formerly been expected

of it. Although many professional educators still believe that through the schools they can reform and
perfect society, most thinking people realize that education only renders students capable of greater good
or evil. Which way this increased potential is to be
used depends on the student's morality, which he
obtains more from his family and church than from
the school.

The intellectual shortcomings of contemporary
education have been a matter of lively discussion in
recent years. The Soviet Union's superiority in
the nuclear-arms and space-penetration races caused
Americans to re-examine their educational system, to
insist on earlier specialization in science, or less time-
wasting in the lower grades, and on dropping "friv-
olous" subjects—which to some people meant Latin
and Greek, to others bridge and sewing. The lively
discussions on how to improve our educational system
in 1959 showed how confused Americans are about
the basic aims of education and the philosophy
underlying it.

We may as well admit that we are at a disadvan-
tage in any short-distance race with the U.S.S.R.
in scientific and technological training. The Soviet
government can begin specialization in the cradle,
and it can guide scientists through educational chan-

nels so specialized that the professional man's competence lies exclusively within his field. He is not allowed to think outside his profession, since there is no need for him to have independent opinions on public policy, aesthetics, religion, the nature of man and of God. These opinions are manufactured for him by the Soviet propaganda machine and handed down to him from above. It is easy to train technological and scientific experts quickly in this system— but there is some question whether it might not have seeds of its own decay when intellectual activity is so completely bureaucratized and when freedom of investigation is narrowly confined to specific projects for research prescribed by political authorities.

If we were to follow such a system, as some urge we do, we would destroy the very way of life we frantically seek to defend. For democratic government ultimately depends upon a sizeable base of liberally educated citizens. If professional and technical specialization begins too soon, if something like Newman's liberal education is not obtained by a sizeable fraction of our citizenry, if these people cannot exercise their minds freely to make balanced judgments and form sound opinions on questions of public policy, then democratic, responsible government takes on a hollow sound.

Recent educational reforms recognize diversity of interest and variety of ability among students. These reforms are a revolt against the attempt previously made by some educators—all of whom are by no means dead—to hammer all students into the same American mold. Many schools have adopted the "track" system offering different curricula to students with different objectives and different abilities. "Advanced learning" programs are being widely adopted for superior students who, it is now generally agreed, should not sit on their books and make spitballs until the average and inferior students catch up with them. The track system and advanced learning programs are doing something to get the better students into specialized learning at an earlier stage without entirely eliminating those subjects which have traditionally been part of a liberal education.

Liberal education dies hard. Its demise has been announced periodically ever since Socrates tutored Plato in the liberal atmosphere of Athens. But liberal education, like Huck Finn and Mark Twain, has been privileged to attend its own funeral—and further even to attend the funerals of its pallbearers. In this last century it has been buried by utilitarians and progressivists—but somehow it survives. It carries with it a bagful rather than a libraryful of books, and these have become the subject matter of Great Books Courses in colleges and adult study groups throughout the country. It has tried to work out a treaty of co-existence with the modern world whereby it becomes a voluntary adjunct to specialized training for those who think it worth the time and effort required to obtain it.

One can imagine Socrates pausing under a tree as he and Plato perambulated about Athens, grasping Plato's elbow and saying with deep feeling: "Young man, Greek education is in critical condition. Sophists, cynics, and other intellectual shams have wormed their way into our educational system. Unless we reform things thoroughly the Greek ideal of education will be lost in oblivion." Thus it has gone through the history of education, with the liberal curriculum facing one crisis after another. Only dates and labels change. The basic issue persists. Today efficiency experts, IBM machines, college administrators, and alumni benefactors seem to have replaced the sophists and cynics of Plato's youth.

But, we say, liberal education has a way of surviving its pallbearers. In recent years personnel managers of some large and successful concerns say they are interested in liberally educated young men who can obtain their technical training on the job and go on to become successful executives because they have developed an "intellect, which has been disciplined to the perfection of its powers, which knows, and thinks while it knows, which has learned to leaven the dense mass of facts and events with the elastic force of reason, which discerns the end in every beginning, the origin in every end, the law in every interruption, the limit in each delay, which knows where it stands, and how its path lines from one point to another."

Spencer's and Dewey's influence on education is not to be denied or minimized, but the ideal propounded by Newman in *The Idea of a University* has by no means been extinguished.

Chapter VIII

Conclusion: Speed and Space

IT IS a mistake to think that ideas are everything in history, just as it is wrong to ignore them. An argument could go on forever about the relative influence on the modern world of Charles Darwin and Henry Maudsley. We have seen that Darwin's contribution was considerable, and hundreds of conferences are being held in 1959 to commemorate the significance of his work in 1859. Maudsley has fallen into obscurity. But economic historians do not forget that he invented the lathe, which made possible absolute accuracy and therewith interchangeable parts, thus creating modern machinery and the industrial system. One can properly maintain that had there been no Darwin and no Maudsley there would still have been a theory of evolution by survival of the fittest and our present industrial economy. But the fact is that we have had a Darwin and a Maudsley, and to them we can properly attribute the results of their discoveries. Intelligent men will allow that a case can be made for each one's greater importance, and that wisdom requires acknowledging that neither should be ignored.

Symbolic of the importance of 1859 is the discovery of the first commercial oil field in Pennsylvania and the introduction of tungsten steel into Germany. For in the century since 1859, industrial development has centered around oil and steel. There is no need here to detail the progress of the industrialization of the world in the last century. Suffice it to remind ourselves that every country in the world, with the possible exception of England, was basically agricultural a century ago, that as a result of the industrial and agricultural revolution of the last century all parts of the Western world except some Latin American countries have become primarily industrial. With this change has come urbanization and its attendant problems of broken homes, juvenile delinquency, slum areas, and increased crime caused by packing people like olives in a jar into urban areas. Industrialization caused new class alignments, increased the wealth of the world unbelievably, and in many ways changed the very face of the earth.

Here we are interested with a single aspect of industrialization and its relation to the subjects of the preceding essays: the increased rate of acceleration since 1859. A generation earlier George Stephenson's "Rocket" had been clocked at the unbelievable speed of 31 miles an hour—and many had doubted that man could maintain life at that speed. He did. Soon he was driving steam locomotives more than twice that fast, and in our day he is flying through space at a greater speed than sound and preparing to hurtle himself into outer space at a speed which almost defies imagination. This accelerated speed does not leave man unaffected. Moreover, it is symbolic of the rate of change and flux in all life, from ladies' fashions to communications, from ideas and modes of thought to styles of architecture. In such an age of flux as we have reached, yesterday seems in the distant past and today seems slipping out of reach, as tomorrow seems uncertain, inviting, but threatening.

One prevalent note in this age of flux has been the Western world's tendency to repudiate its past. Liberals have consistently tried to cut loose from what they consider the burden of history, to break through the cake of custom into a free society rationally planned. Many social and political experiments have been tried since 1859, and most of them have been found wanting. Repudiation of the past has involved a movement called "secularization," whereby the Western world has with each decade "pushed God farther off"—as Emma Darwin complained each of her husband's books did.

Running counter to this general process of repudiating the past and secularizing life has been a hard core of religious and political conservatism, which has grown stronger in the last two decades as it adapted itself to inevitable change in the hope of controlling it. Conservatives do not oppose change. They only insist that it must be slow, gradual, "organic" rather than revolutionary and unconditioned by the past. Conservatives prize what endures in history, like the family and the land and the Church, while merely tolerating change as one of the unpleasant facts of life.

History is a story of change and persistance. Through the centuries new institutions, ideas, and relations are born, while old ones die. Meanwhile some things perdure. Among these is human nature itself, for man has proven himself tougher and more resilient this last century than philosophers and physiologists thought him to be. There is more rubber in man than social theorists suspect. Despite theories to the contrary, most men have a way of letting human nature break through the shell of theory in which it has been encased by men like Spencer and

Darwin. To put it another way, mankind saves itself by not logically and completely putting into practice the theories of the last century—as Nazis did in hospitals and concentration camps in Germany and the lands they conquered.

So it is with ideas and systems of thought. Some of the ideas we have examined in the preceding pages have been repudiated and have lost their appeal. Others are still influential, modified by a century of history to be sure, but nonetheless still alive and vigorous. Among these latter, Darwinism and Marxism are perhaps the most important in 1959. Neither Darwin's *Origin* nor Marx's *Critique of Political Economy* has weathered the criticism of men and events in the last hundred years, but the cluster of ideas each book presents has done much to remake the modern world, and will continue in modified form to be influential in the coming century.

Some ideas have been repudiated. The Liberalism of Samuel Smiles has been criticized on moral, economic, social, and political grounds. It has proved unworkable, and it has given way to an entirely different and contradictory form of Liberalism, that of the Welfare State. It is still defended by a small group who shrill out their warnings about the terrors of security and "socialism," but they are defending an empty castle from which the last breath of life has long since departed.

Nationalism survived the first World War and reached its most perfervid form in Fascism and Nazism, but it failed in the Western world to survive the debacle of the second World War. Europeans recovered from this second shock treatment to see how absurd and dangerous was this secular religion of hate. The germs of nationalism may have been destroyed in the body of the Western world by the last war—if we may change metaphor—but they had previously escaped to infect the Asiatic and African peoples. Nationalism has been on the increase in these areas, and there is no reason to expect it to subside in the foreseeable future.

A third bundle of ideas and practices, imperialism, has also been repudiated. Imperialism has acted like the perennial boomerang in comic strips. In the first square it was thrown into space by the European world. In the middle squares it brought glory and gold to the European nations. But in the last square it is hitting Europe in the back of the head with shaking, traumatic effects.

Education and liberty are problems as old as the human race. Statements made in 1859 have not resolved the problems, but they are among the most important formulations of both problem and answer in modern times. Neither Spencer's or Newman's system of education nor Mill's case for liberty can stand unmodified in our technological age, but all three suggest lines of thought that can well serve as points of departure for fresh thinking on these problems in 1959.

Newman described the liberally educated person as one who, from his knowledge of history, is almost prophetic in his view of the future. Historians shun this as too large a claim, for the events of tomorrow are quite careless of what we say about them today. Historians prefer to claim another quality of the liberal mind described by Newman as "equitableness" and "tranquility." For a study of men's thought and action in the past shows that contemporaries considered every age one of crisis, and there were always those who believed that the end was at hand. But human nature has had a way of surviving. This last century has seen changes unlike any previous hundred years, and acceleration in all phases of life has increased at a rate that only a young Jules Verne could imagine in 1859. Nevertheless, modern man seems likely to create from new techniques such

protective devices as will enable him to enter the
coming century with the odds in favor of his survival
—and perhaps even his sanity.

A NOTE ON THE TYPE

IN WHICH THIS BOOK IS SET

This book is set in Fairfield, a Linotype face, created by Rudolph Ruzicka, distinguished American artist and engraver. Introduced in 1940, Fairfield is almost strictly a book type with much charm and beauty. It is easy to read as one learns from extensive reading since it furnishes some degree of stimulation and pleasure to the eye. The fitting of each letter is practically perfect, which is a real tribute to its designer. This book was composed by Progressive Typographers, Inc., of York, Pa., printed by the Wickersham Printing Company of Lancaster, Pa. and bound by Moore and Company of Baltimore, Md. The typography and design are by Howard N. King.

Date Due

	PRINTED	IN U. S. A.	